BOTTOMS UP

A RECOVERY

BOTTOMS UP

A RECOVERY

by Paul C.

Hotchkiss Publishing

2016

ISBN 978-0-9909020-5-8
Library of Congress Control Number: 2016954404

First edition: July 2016 by Notch Publishing
Second Edition: October 2016 by Hotchkiss Publishing

Designed by: Eugene Michalenko
Cover photo & design by: Paul Clermont

HOTCHKISS PUBSLISHING
17 Frank Street
Branford, CT 06405
info@hotchkisspublishing.com
www.hotchkisspublishing.com

For the alcoholic who still suffers,
inside and outside of the rooms.

CONTENTS

WHAT IT'S LIKE NOW

INTRODUCTION

This book was written by a sober member of Alcoholics Anonymous who was approaching the end of his life. He wanted to write his story down so that others might benefit from his experience, strength, and hope.

I married Paul, the author of this book, in 1966. I was only 18 years old and he was 21. We had an amicable divorce after 35 years of marriage and we continued a close friendship until his death in 2016.

In the first 13 years of my marriage to Paul, neither one of us realized that he was an alcoholic. Yes, he drank too often, and way too much.

There were numerous times he didn't come home until after the bars closed. I lived in fear on those nights, terrified that he would get into an accident, harming himself or possibly others. Even when he walked through the door and I knew he was safe, I was still fearful. I never knew what to expect. I walked on eggshells because the slightest thing could incite an argument between us. All of my tearful pleading and ultimatums were ignored. I believed that if he really loved me and our children he would simply stop drinking. How hard was that? My husband could not be depended upon to be there for us. By the time Paul hit rock bottom, we were both broken and in need of help. Fortunately, we found our way to a 12-Step way of life: Alcoholics Anonymous for Paul, and Al-Anon for me. In these two programs we found the tools, the love and the support to help Paul achieve sobriety and to help me restore my sanity. We were able to grow and integrate a wonderful set of principles into our daily lives.

Paul completed "Bottoms Up" during the late stages of a terminal illness. He was in a great deal of pain and dependent on oxygen, but he wrote every day, absolutely determined to get his book written and published before it was too late. He had a real commitment to helping others, the way some had reached out to help him. Writing this book was one last way for Paul to pay forward what was freely given to him.

Even with a death sentence hanging over him, I witnessed his calm acceptance of his illness. I never saw any evidence of him feeling sorry for himself. In fact he wrote his own obituary (see: In Memory p. 109). He only had gratitude for his sobriety and the life he had because of it. The day after his books arrived from the printer he took a turn for the worse and was taken by ambulance to a hospice house. He passed away a few days later.

Every time I pick up this book, I can't help but stare at the image on the cover. It tugs at my heart. Paul and I were together the day he took that photo. He was only a year or two sober when he took it; it shows a man acknowledging him by lifting his bottle and giving my husband a silent toast. It shook Paul to the very core of his being. He had a glimpse of the future he would have had if he had not found sobriety.

Paul was a gifted A.A. speaker and storyteller, whose stories never failed to move and inspire the people he helped. This book allowed Paul to tell his story of recovery one last time. I am hopeful that, through this book, Paul will remain a helpful companion to people recovering from alcoholism. If there's anything in this book that inspires you, makes you think, or assists your recovery in any way, I know Paul would be delighted. The only thing he'd ask you to do in return is: Pass it on.

Cheryl C.

AUTHOR'S NOTE

Each time I speak at or chair a meeting of Alcoholics Anonymous, I begin with the following words:

"My name is _____ and I am an alcoholic. My sobriety date is February 15, 1979, and I always remind myself that it is an honor and a privilege to chair or speak at an Alcoholics Anonymous meeting. Thank you for asking me."

I have been diagnosed with Pulmonary Fibrosis, a terminal respiratory disease, which has no connection to my alcoholism. According to my doctors, I may have from a few months up to one year before I reach my earthly expiration date. At this writing I am a bit past the halfway mark in completing this book. If you are reading this, then I did indeed finish it.

As a member of Alcoholics Anonymous I have endeavored to pass along the gift of sobriety to other alcoholics for almost 38 years. I hope this book will continue to do the same.

As my A.A. sponsor Joel often said: "It's only life and death; try not to take it too seriously."

WHAT IT WAS LIKE

I was in trouble with alcohol the summer that I graduated from high school at age 17. Yet, despite the experiences documented here that give a few insights as to what life is like for a functioning alcoholic, I still continued to drink.

During the ensuing years my disease and I would manage to severely corrupt or abandon whatever principles of decency I may have possessed. I rarely if ever had a problem with morally or ethically questionable decisions. When faced with those dilemmas, at almost every instance, I would lower my standards. I would, like most alcoholics, eventually become a master of rationalization, denial and deceit.

Opting instead to drink, I would continue to compromise my integrity and abandon many of my responsibilities until I reluctantly arrived at a meeting of Alcoholics Anonymous 17 years later.

THE MAN IN THE WALL
STREETER SHOES

I was eight years old when I saw my first death caused by alcoholism. An invitation to my aunt and uncle's for a Saturday afternoon spaghetti supper meant good food. On this hot summer afternoon in 1952, it would mean a whole lot more.

My aunt and uncle's apartment was upstairs over a drugstore on a busy downtown street corner. While the spaghetti sauce simmered in the kitchen and the adults visited, there was always time to admire the exotic souvenirs that were displayed in their home.
A miniature Statue of Liberty stood on the breakfront next to the dial phone. An engraved ebony pool cue sent from Korea by one of their sons hung over the sofa.

Even a visit to the bathroom was interesting. Once inside I'd lock the door and quietly take the bathrobes off the door revealing a Vargas calendar. I'd be looking at Miss October or November before someone would knock to ask if I was ever coming out.

"Honey," my uncle called to his wife, "I'm out of cigarettes, so I'll skip over to Dodd's and get a pack." "Don't be too long, I'm setting the table," she replied. "You want to come along?" he asked me. "You bet," I answered.

A visit to Dodd's Tavern was better than being roped into helping set the table. And there was always the likely possibility that my uncle would have a quick beer and buy me a coke in the bargain.

Dodd's wasn't far away. It was a neighborhood watering hole about three doors up the street. As usual in the summer, the door was propped open. You didn't need any shrewd powers of observation to detect what was different in Dodd's that afternoon.

"What the hell happened?" my uncle asked. As the guys at the bar were telling him, my eyes were riveted on the man who was lying on the two tables that had been put together. They were those square, black pedestal tables with chrome edges. His legs bent at the knees hung over the edge, and his face had been covered with a small white towel (more commonly called a bar-rag). I kept looking at him. He was dead! He had just given up the ghost right there at the bar. The regulars were speculating as to what had caused his demise. "Aw, he had a bum ticker." "This heat's enough to kill anybody." "It's that gin he always drank, it gets your nervous system." As they toasted his memory and the bartender announced that he was going to put his stool in the back room for a week out of respect. I noticed the dead man's shoes. I'd never seen a cadaver before and I'd never seen shoes like that either. They were Wall Streeter wing-tips and they were polished to perfection. As if they'd read my thoughts, the boys at the bar started talking about how the deceased had always worn Wall Streeters.

Like my uncle, the dead man and many of Dodd's customers worked at the Wall Streeter Shoe Company on Union Street. The men at the bar were wagering as to who would admire fine footwear more, St. Peter or Lucifer, when my uncle and I left. We both squinted as we emerged from the darkened interior of Dodd's and walked out into the late afternoon sunlight.

As we turned back towards their apartment, my uncle pulled a Lucky out of his fresh pack. "Who was that man?" I asked "Just another working stiff."... His laughter cracked and he coughed as he exhaled. "He worked with me at the shoe shop. It's too bad, he was an all-right guy who had a lot of tough breaks."

When we reached the doorway that led upstairs to my aunt and uncle's apartment, he took a last drag on his Lucky Strike and flipped the butt into the gutter. As the cigarette landed, he was taking his handkerchief out of his pants pocket.

He paused a moment "Smell that!" he said. The aroma of my aunt's spaghetti sauce drifted down the stairs. The clatter of dishes, sounds of conversations and my aunt's laughter filled the hallway. "You know your aunt makes the best damn spaghetti sauce in the whole county. Sometimes I forget that," he said. He wiped the tears away with the crumpled up handkerchief and stuffed it into his back pocket as we walked up the stairs.

EASTER SUNDAY

I was sixteen and she was fifteen. My ethnic heritage was French, hers Polish. We had been going steady for several months when she invited me to her house for Easter dinner. Easter Sunday was a very important religious holiday in the Polish community of the small town where we lived. I knocked on the front door and Vicki ushered me into a kitchen filled with cooking aromas that made my mouth water. Immediately to the right of the kitchen door stood the Easter dinner table; it had been set that morning so it would be ready when the parish priest arrived to offer his Easter blessing. It was resplendent with linens, flatware, plates, glasses and a large basket filled with *Babka* (a traditional Easter raisin-bread) and at the center the *Baranek* a Pascal lamb (carved of butter, with cloves for eyes, and holding a tiny red banner emblazoned with a cross).

The kitchen was already crowded with Vicki's parents and her three siblings. Several aunts, uncles and cousins had arrived right after I did with a few more coming in shortly after. The parish priest showed up in plenty of time to bless the Easter feast. As the women helped one another with last minute cooking chores, the men sat in the living room drinking *Jeżynówka*, a blackberry brandy, with beer chasers. After the men were coaxed back into the kitchen by the women, everyone sat at the table and we began to feast on such delicacies as: *kiełbasa* served with homemade horseradish that made your eyes water, *gołąbki* (cabbage leaves stuffed with hamburger rice), *pierogi* (dumplings filled with cheese and potato), and *kapusta* (a mixture of cabbage, corn, pork and spices).

Unfortunately the priest's blessing and all of that great food wasn't enough to overcome the effects of the brandy and beer that had been consumed by the men before and during dinner. As the women began clearing the table, one of Vicki's inebriated uncles picked up the Pascal lamb, who was now missing one of its clove eyes and a good deal of its buttery fleece, and hurled it at her father, offering a curse in Polish as he did. The kitchen fell silent for a moment as Vicki's mom picked up the deformed lamb and the miraculously unbroken butter dish off the floor. The silence ended when Vicki's father cold-cocked the cursing uncle, who landed on the floor just inches from where the lamb had been. Then all hell broke loose.

The men started throwing drunken punches and yelling curses at each other in Polish and English. One of the combatants fell against the refrigerator door, and his bloody nose left a red streak of blood as he slid down to the floor. Two of the men collided with the kitchen table, sending the few remaining dishes crashing to the floor. The screaming of the women finally brought the fighting to an end. The men quietly staggered into the living-room, leaving the one uncle at the base of the refrigerator, blacked out, his nose still bleeding. As his sobbing wife was tending to his rum blossom of a nose, she turned to the other women and asked plaintively; "How could this happen on Easter Sunday?"

I guess everyone in that kitchen including me missed the fact that alcohol might have been the fuel that ignited the fracas. Alcohol would continue to ruin many holidays for Vicki's family and mine as well in the years to come.

LIFEGUARD

I had graduated from high school two weeks before I started my job as a lifeguard at a summer camp for boys. It was run by Jesuit priests on a lush and expansive campus that served as an exclusive preparatory school during the rest of the calendar year. To reach the private beach on the small lake to swim the campers walked down a winding footpath under a canopy of maple and elm trees, crossing a two-lane county highway, through the parking lot of the Raoul Club, and down to the lake. It was the Raoul Club that would prove to be the beginning my undoing.

Someone on the camp staff had determined that four lifeguards were required to insure the safety of the young swimmers. The cool, dark inviting interior of the Raoul Club and its sign advertising "delicious cheese dinner rolls" was a temptation that grew harder to resist every time I walked past with my young aquatic charges. In order to take advantage of the Raoul Club's enticing offer of cool drinks and cheese rolls, I calculated that two lifeguards would provide adequate safety and supervision while the campers swam in the lake. In truly democratic fashion, I put my idea up to a vote with the other three lifeguards; two of them readily agreed that it was truly inspired; the third was less enthusiastic but reluctantly went along with the major- ity. We agreed to draw straws to determine who would make the trek down to the beach and which two would peel off at the Raoul Club. Thus began my almost daily elbow-polishing of the mahogany bar and sipping gin and tonics expertly prepared by Madeline the bartender.

Madeline was a tall, nervous and thin fortyish woman with un- ruly, wiry blond hair that stuck out from her head in every direction. Although her vision must have been severely impaired (she wore eye- glasses with what we referred to as "coke bottle" lenses), she kept the gin and tonics coming and always managed to provide us with a few of those famous cheese rolls along with our Beefeater-laced libations. Although we were all underage, she never asked us to produce IDs. "Hell, with my eyes I couldn't read them anyways," she would joke.

It wasn't Madeline and the gin and tonics that proved to be my final undoing at the summer camp; it would come in the form of a blind date, and a fifth (four fifths of a quart-- the liquor industry hadn't gone metric yet) of Canadian Club whiskey. The camp was located about twenty miles from my hometown and my friend Richie had called. He finally had persuaded the girl that he had been pursuing for weeks to go out with him, but only if he could find a date for her cousin Sylvia who was staying at her house for a few weeks. I told him that I wasn't too keen on blind dates, but he insisted that she was a drop-dead gorgeous blonde. I agreed and we made arrangements for them to pick me up at the camp on the following Tuesday, my day off.

Tuesday night came and Richie, Donna, and her cousin Sylvia arrived at the camp in his dad's Buick. Richie hadn't exaggerated one bit; Sylvia "Call me Syd," she said as we were introduced, was indeed a stunning blue eyed blonde dressed in a white tank top and cut-off denim shorts. Richie had brought along the fifth of Canadian Club and asked me where we could go. "The camp has a private beach on the lake and no one will be there at night. We'll have the place to ourselves." I suggested. "Maybe we can go skinny dipping," said Donna. Syd gave me a suggestive smile. *This is going to be some first date*, I thought.

We parked the Buick in a far corner of the Raoul Club's parking lot and walked down the short path that led to the camp's beach. Richie and Donna decided to take a walk along the narrow dirt road that circled the lake. I told Syd that the view of the moonlight shimmering off the lake would be better if we sat on one of the lifeguard towers at either end of the dock. She climbed up first; I followed along with the fifth of CC and started sipping straight from the bottle. The next thing I remember was waking up in my bed the next morning, hungover, my body scraped and bruised, without a clue as to how I'd gotten there. At some point I went into my first alcohol induced blackout. I vaguely remembered falling off of the lifeguard tower. My roommate Pete told me that I had been very adventuresome the night before, and that the priest who was the camp director wanted to see me in his office.

I made myself as presentable as possible and showed up at his office later that morning. He was brief and to the point. "Your drunken behavior last night has been brought to my attention by several of the staff members. We do not tolerate such behavior here. I am relieving you of your duties as a lifeguard and you are to be off campus by three this afternoon. I tried to utter some lame excuse that would save me, but the priest wasn't interested. He waved his hand in a dismissive gesture and pointed toward the door.

I used the phone in his outer office to call my parents. I made up a barely plausible lie that the job wasn't a good fit and that I had decided to find a summer job back in my hometown. I walked back to my room and silently began to pack.

This would be the first of many consequences I would pay because of my drinking, and I would continue paying for the next seventeen years. Sadly, members of my family and many of my friends would innocently pay consequences as well.

In the book Twelve Steps and Twelve Traditions (known as the Twelve and Twelve in A. A. parlance), the second paragraph of Step One describes alcohol as "the rapacious creditor." Rapacious is defined by Mr. Webster as plundering, greedy, ravenous, and subsisting on live prey. This summer job would be the first of many things that this relentless creditor would take away from me. Some things, like this job, would be tangible; others far more valuable and important would be taken as well.

DUI

As a teenager I was interested in art, so I attended an exhibit of works by local artists in a nearby city. It was one of those wine and cheese receptions where the room is filled with air kisses and overly complimentary conversations. I drank a lot of the wine, ate a bit of brie, and got more than just an air kiss from an attractive young woman. She said that she didn't live too far away and invited me over to her place for "a nightcap." Although my vision was blurred and my speech slightly slurred, I jumped at the invite.

Her place turned out to be her parent's home in a very upscale part of town; they were away on a business trip and she had the house to herself. We went downstairs into a basement that had been turned into what was then called a "rumpus-room." It was furnished with sofas, overstuffed chairs, television, a jukebox, and a fully stocked bar. We picked out a few tunes on the jukebox, danced a couple of slow dances and then sat down at the bar. She insisted on mixing us up a couple of her favorite cocktails. They were Brandy Alexanders: a combination of brandy, crème de cocoa, and cream all whirred together in a blender and topped with a dash of nutmeg. They didn't taste much like booze and they went down easily, so I had a few. Added to the wine I'd consumed at the art exhibit, they left me in no shape to drive home, but that's exactly what I did. I didn't make it very far. As I approached an intersection three blocks from her house, I crashed into a stop sign, bringing my car to a noisy and abrupt halt. The noise must have awakened a nearby neighbor who called the police; they arrived within minutes of the accident.

The next morning, my memory of what happened the night before was spotty at best. The end result would be my first DUI. Back in the '60s the fines were lower and the length of time your license was suspended shorter. I considered both a minor inconvenience, and rationalized my getting caught a result of a nosy resident who should have minded his or her own business. This would be my first encounter with the legal system as a result of my drinking. It would not be my last.

MRS. B'S

She was a dipso-divorcee, the eternal victim of the husband who had left her for another woman, an elected town official, the mother of one of my high school classmates and our drinking buddy. It was the mid '60s and I was attending college 150 miles from home. I usually made it home on weekends. And of course I was back in my home town for the summer months, as were her daughter and many of our high school friends.

Mrs. B lived in a modest brick ranch house on a street that turned into a state highway. At least once a week or so, a few of us politically astute, and morally concerned pseudo-intellectuals would gather at Mrs. B's to discuss and debate the world's problems and offer our insightful solutions.

Mrs. B's choice of beverage was Ballantine Beer which she drank out of quart bottles, one of which was always conveniently at hand on the floor next to her favorite living-room chair. The rest of us drank whatever we could illegally obtain because the legal drinking age in our state was 21. The spirited discussions and verbal repartee would continue on into the early hours of the morning. The decibel level rising in direct correlation to the amount of beer and whiskey we consumed. One of our favorite topics for debate and discussion was the Vietnam War. The mid-to-late '60s were a time of antiwar demonstrations, draft card burnings and draft dodgers fleeing to Canada. The evening TV news featured picketers outside of military induction centers, gory footage from Southeast Asia and protesters marching in front of the White House. These scenes served as fodder for our alcohol-laced young liberal views.

As I write this an old quote comes to mind: "If you're young and not a liberal, then you have no heart. If you're old and not a conservative, then you have no brain." We were liberal all right and had plenty of heart, but the booze we consumed certainly didn't enhance whatever brain power we might have possessed.

On a few of these alcohol fueled evenings, usually at around two or three in the morning someone would come up with the idea that we ought to do something about this horrible war. The slightly slurred suggestions that followed varied. Most were nebulous thoughts on how we could end the war in Vietnam. Even in an alcoholic induced haze we knew that we couldn't do a hell of a lot about effectively ending the war. On at least one or two occasions someone (it might have even been me) would ask: "Why not take our concerns right to the top?" "Yeah, let's call the White House!" others would agree.

Back in the '60s, in the age of dial phones and live operators, calling the White House wasn't difficult at all. You simply dialed "0" for the operator and asked for information. Once the information operator came on the line you simply gave her the address and name of the person whose number you wanted and she would provide the number.

Once we had the number, our collective liquid courage had no problem in dialing 1600 Pennsylvania Avenue. Even in the ungodly hours of the early morning a White House operator would answer the phone. "This is the White House. How may I direct your call?" Encouraged by our background support, whoever held the receiver would ask to speak to President Johnson. The White House operator would graciously respond: "The President is not available at this time. May I take a message?" We would collectively respond: We want him to end this (pick an obscene adjective or an adverb) war! The operator would respond in a perfect unemotional monotone: "I will be sure to relay your message to the President."

On the next day, once our hangovers had vanished, we would proudly boast about how we had called the White House and left a message for the President about ending the war in Vietnam. On hearing of our telephone bravado, some of our friends would give us an admiring "Way to go!" Others would shake their heads in disbelief and tell us how stupid and disrespectful we were.

I strongly suspect that if anyone places a 2 or 3 a.m. call to the White House these days, they would be met by more than "Atta boys!" or disapproving looks the next day. They would, more than likely, have the Secret Service or FBI knocking at the door wanting to ask them a few questions.

OVER THE LINE

The state line was only 12 miles away as the crow flies. That 12 miles of narrow two-lane road passed through rural farm country and a few small towns and led to the Empire State, New York, where drinking was legal at age 18. Once you crossed the border you didn't have to travel far before you reached several gin mills and road houses that catered to us teenaged drinkers. Any half-assed fake ID was readily accepted by the bouncers and bartenders at most of these watering holes.

Mine was a Rhode Island driver's permit. One of our high school classmates had stolen a pad of permits from a registry office in Providence. Since there was no photo required all we had to do was have one of the girls in typing class type in the information on the permit. I was a history buff, so I adopted the alias of Samuel Flagg Bemis, a noted historical writer. My physical description and a date of birth making me 18 were filled in and I was ready to go. The New York State bars I was to frequent for the next several years were ready for me too. They had names that ranged from those of their owners: Hayden's, Uncle Ken's, and Saluzzo's to The Three Way, The Top Hat and The Five Flies. The Three Way was the first roadhouse you came to after crossing the state line. I had a couple of friends who played in the house band on Friday and Saturday nights so it was always my first choice for a night "over the line."

It was a night that began at The Three Way that would end in my first time behind bars. I'd been chatting up and dancing with one of two girls when my best friend Roger, who sang and played guitar with the band, came over to the table where we were sitting when the band took a break. The girls told us that they were staying in a cottage at a nearby lake and asked if we'd like to go skinny dipping with them after The Three Way closed. We couldn't wait 'til 3 a.m. We bought a couple of six-packs from Tommy the bartender on the way out. "Just follow us, it's only about 10 miles," the girls called out. I wasn't about to lose them so I stayed right on their bumper. Just outside the village of Hoosick Falls I asked Roger to pop open a couple of beers.

We were only about three miles from the lake and were grinning like Cheshire cats as I accelerated up the steep hill that led out of the village. That's when the red lights of the police cruiser started flashing in my rear-view-mirror. I pulled over. The girls kept going.

As their taillights disappeared, I frantically told Roger, "Hide the beer." I rolled down the side window as the burly village cop walked up to the side of my Mustang. "Did you know you were tailgating that car pretty close?" He sneered. *If you were me you'd be tailgating that car too*, I thought. "License and registration," he demanded. As I was reaching into the glove-compartment for the registration, he scanned the interior of the car with his flashlight. He put Roger's face dead center in the beam of light and asked, "What you got on the floor there 'neath your legs?" Roger smiled sheepishly as he uncrossed his legs revealing two cans of Budweiser. "Well boys, looks like you're in violation of the open container law." He quickly ordered Roger out of the car, handcuffed him, placed him in the backseat of the cruiser and seized the two cans of beer. He then ordered me to turn my car around and follow him to town hall.

When we arrived he ordered me out of the car and confiscated the remaining 10 cans of beer. He marched us inside and downstairs to the police department's dingy office, where a cop wearing captain's bars sat at an old beat up metal desk. "What have we got here, Sergeant Harrison?" he asked. "A couple a beatniks tailgating and drinking beer." He grinned.

"Did he just call us beatniks?" I whispered to Roger.

"Okay. I'll call the J.P.," the captain said. Calling the Justice of the Peace at 3:30 a.m. meant that we were going to be tried in what we sarcastically called Kangaroo Court. That's when you were hauled before a small town Justice of the Peace usually found guilty and summarily fined or jailed, depending on the offense. The captain got off the phone and announced that the J.P would be there in about 10 minutes. Roger and I sat on a wooden bench and silently waited while Sergeant Harrison kept asking the captain questions on how to fill out the arrest forms. Turned out that the Hoosick Falls police force consisted of three policemen, the chief, a captain and the rookie who was our arresting officer.

True to his word the Justice of the Peace walked in exactly ten minutes later. Sgt. Harrison jumped to his feet and proudly pointed to us. "Here they are, your Honor." Justice Thomas Rustino looked me in the eye, and to the astonishment of Roger and the cops, called me by my first name and said, "Why don't we step outside for a moment." In addition to being an elected Justice of the Peace, Tommy Rustino owned and operated the filling station next to the bridge in Hoosick Falls. He was also a golfing buddy of Linda's father. I had dated Linda for several months the previous year and had gotten to know and like Tommy. Fortunately, he liked me too.

"What are they charging you with?" he asked.

"Violating the open container law," I answered.

"Well look, here's what I'll do, when we go back in tell your buddy to plead guilty. I'll sentence you to a night in jail. Hell, it's almost four a.m. already. They'll release you at 7 and you'll probably even get your beer back."

"Wow, thanks a lot Tommy," I smiled.

"Just remember, when we go back inside, I'm Judge Rustino, not Tommy."

We walked back inside and Judge Rustino walked over to Roger and explained what he was going to do for us. "I can't spend the night in jail." Roger cried. "My father would kill me!"

"Okay, I'll fine you $25.00 dollars and release you."

"But I don't have the $25.00." Roger pleaded. "And how am I going to get back to The Three Way and get my car?"

"Christ Roger, the judge is doing us a big favor, quit complaining or you'll screw this up." I whispered.

The Judge then reassured Roger, "You can come back within 48 hours and pay the fine, and I'll even give you a ride to The Three Way. I'm going over to Sgt. Harrison to get the paper work and court will be in session shortly." Judge Rustino gave us a reassuring wink.

A few minutes later we were led upstairs into a large well appointed office. Judge Rustino was seated behind a large carved oak desk. He rapped the desktop with a small gavel. "Court's in session," he announced. "I see by Officer Harrison's report that you both are charged with violating the open container statute. How do you plead?"

"Guilty, your Honor," we replied in unison. Pointing at me, he loudly announced that he was sentencing me to one night in the Hoosick Falls jail. He turned toward Roger, "And you I'm going to fine $25.00. I'll give you 48 hours to remit that amount to the town clerk."

Sgt. Harrison interrupted. "That's it; that's all you're going to …"

Judge Rustino cut him off. "Look Sgt. Harrison, I make the decisions here. You remain quiet and listen."

"Yes, your Honor." He blushed. And with that court was adjourned.

Tommy gave Roger a ride back to The Three Way as I began my night of incarceration in the Hoosick Falls lockup. The basement cells were painted a blinding white. My cell contained a narrow bed and a blanket so stiff and dirty I could have stood it up in the corner.

I was released promptly at 7 a.m. next morning. When I got home my father asked where the hell I'd been all night. I told him what had happened and he came back with the usual tirade about my going to Hoosick Falls, and that I should stay in my hometown.

Roger returned on Monday and paid his fine. The end of the story came about a week later. The local newspaper had picked up the police report from two states away. The headline read:

One Jailed One Fined in Hoosick Falls Drinking Incident.

I called Roger. "Did your father see today's paper yet?"

"Yeah," Roger replied.

"Well, what did he say?" I asked.

He said, "You god-damned fool; why didn't you stay in jail?"

COMING TO IN DIXIE

I woke up (or should I say came to) in a room in the Dixie Hotel just off Times Square in New York City. It was January, and the single large window was wide-open, snow was blowing in, and I was wrapped up in the drapes that had been torn down. There were a dozen or so persons asleep or unconscious lying on the twin beds, on the floor, or slouched in chairs. One of the men had a physician's bag clutched in his arms. I knew instinctively that he wasn't a doctor. All of these people were total strangers to me save one: Charlie, who was passed out on the floor next to me, was a Brooklyn native and we had set out several hours earlier to go night clubbing in Manhattan.

We started out in the early evening having a couple of scotches at the Metropole Café on the corner of 7th Avenue and 48th Street where Gene Krupa, a long over the hill drummer was going through the motions on a stage behind the bar. We left the Metropole Café and headed to the Peppermint Lounge on West 45th Street. It had gained popularity along with the twist dance craze made popular by the resident band Joey Dee & The Starliters. The club was frequented by the likes of Frank Sinatra, Norman Mailer, and Marilyn Monroe, and it was even rumored, the elusive Greta Garbo. However none of the glitterati were present during our brief visit. We didn't know it then, but at that time the club was run by Matty "The Horse" Ianiello, a member of the Genovese crime family. We didn't encounter any of those nefarious celebrities either. Later that year the club closed when it lost its liquor license.

It went rapidly downhill from there. We hadn't started out with a whole lot of money and after hitting a few less reputable establishments, we were sneaking into night clubs, finding a table with some empty champagne glasses on it and slowly pouring beer into them from the bottles we had hidden in the pockets of our overcoats.

I can vaguely remember us being thrown out of more than one club before I found myself dancing with a dark and sultry (or at least I thought she was sultry) woman with a heavy Spanish accent in a dimly lit cabaret. Charlie had passed out and was sitting at a corner table with his head resting on his folded coat. When I'd finished dancing with the lovely señorita, Charlie lifted his head and suggested we get the hell out of there. It was probably the sanest idea that either of us had come with all night. By the time we staggered out of that club, I was somehow functioning in a blackout. The next thing I remember is coming to in that room littered with fellow drunks in the Dixie Hotel. I shook Charlie awake and we stumbled down the hallway to the elevator, out through the lobby and into the frosty morning. Charlie, through chattering teeth said: "I'm going to catch a subway to Brooklyn. You want to come over and have some breakfast?"

"No, I've got to get back to school tomorrow morning so I'll be heading back home myself." We gave each other one of those weak smiles that drunks flash when they've survived yet another misadventure.

Home for me was about 150 miles north of New York City. I made my way to the West Side Highway, stamped my feet to ward off the cold, hunched down inside my coat and watched my breath as I exhaled in the cold winter air. I stood shivering as I stuck out my thumb and began hitchhiking my way home.

WINE IN A TAXI

It was February; it was snowing and cold as hell. I had run into Sue at a party a week earlier and she told me that she had moved to an apartment in a town fifteen miles south of where I lived. "Here's my phone number, why don't you give me a call and come over some night," she offered as she handed me a piece of paper. Sue had these large rootbeer-brown eyes that made her suggestion of a visit to her apartment irresistible.

My car was in for repairs and I hadn't been able to beg or borrow one, so I had to hitchhike to her town. We had spent the earlier part of the evening listening to records, sipping wine, and munching on some spicy hors d'oeuvres that she had prepared. Washing down the hors d'oeuvres with plenty of wine was a great excuse for me to slosh down a lot of it rather than slowly sip. We were drinking from the third or fourth bottle at about the time we should have been headed into her bedroom. I was too drunk to do anything once I got there, so she not so politely suggested we call it a night. As I reluctantly prepared to leave, I smuggled what was left of the last bottle of wine out inside of my army-surplus jacket to fortify me against the cold wind that was now fiercely blowing the snow around and dropping the temperature down to single digits. *How could she send me out into this, that cruel bitch?* I thought as I headed down her street.

At the corner a taxi was slowly driving through the white-out that the wind had whipped up. It was over a mile to the corner where I could thumb a ride home, so I tried to wave down the cab. Somehow he saw me trying to flag him down and he pulled over. I hopped into the back seat and told him that I only needed to get to the intersection of Route 8, about a mile away. "No problem." He said. When we got to the intersection he told me that the fare was $10.00. Already pissed at being tossed out into the snow and not curled up in a nice warm bed with Sue, I protested "That's outrageous! I won't pay you ten bucks for a three minute ride."

"You'll pay it or else," he replied.

"How about I just cave in your fuckin' skull!" I threatened as

I pulled the half-full bottle of wine from inside my jacket. His eyes widened as he stuttered, "Okay, okay, take it easy buddy." As he drove away he rolled down his window and yelled that he was going to call the cops. If he did, I got a ride before they showed up.

My excessive drinking had turned a romantic evening that should have ended with me in Sue's warm bed with her arms wrapped around me while I whispered in her ear, to me screaming and threatening a cab driver and slapping my arms to ward off the cold as I tried to thumb a ride on a dark, windswept night in February.

I would see Sue again many years later in a supermarket parking lot while working on my ninth step.

CAPE COD VACATIONS

For several summers in the mid-1970's, when the kid's ages were still in single digits, my wife and I rented a cottage on Cape Cod. The summer of 1975 is more memorable than the others.

Preparing for the long drive to the Cape was an involved process. Clothing for an entire week had to be selected and packed. Bathing suits, beachwear, robes, shorts, sheets and towels, t-shirts, sunscreen, and board games and playing cards for the one inevitable rainy day. But Dad had one indispensable item that had to be carefully stowed with the vacation essentials; a fifth of Tanqueray gin. Although Cape Cod had more than its share of what we called "package stores" where you could buy any kind of liquor, I wasn't taking any chances. The Tanqueray was wrapped in a bath towel and safely tucked inside a picnic basket. God forbid that it would somehow be broken on the journey.

Arrival at the cottage was always a noisy and chaotic event. Unpacking the car and getting everything organized inside the cabin while the kids were already clamoring to go to the beach was nerve racking to say the least. After making sure that my Tanqueray was safely tucked away in one of the kitchen cupboards, I reluctantly took the kids to the nearby beach while my wife finished making the cottage "ours" for the next seven days.

My wife had asked me to stop at the local market and pick up a few things on the way back from the beach, a few basics so she could prepare dinner. She had her priorities, and I had mine: two fresh limes, a bag of ice and three or four quarts of Schweppes tonic water. I couldn't wait to set up my lawn chair and relax in the rays of the late afternoon sun with a cool gin and tonic. I could already feel that icy glass in my hand, beads of condensation trickling over my fingers as I took that first long sip.

When we got back to the cottage, the kids piled out of the car and ran inside telling my wife how much fun the beach was and how they couldn't wait to go again the next day. While they were inside showing my wife the shells they had found, I was outside setting up a folding lawn chair in eager anticipation of enjoying that gin and tonic. "Come on in, I want you to help with dinner," my wife yelled to me from the porch. *When does my vacation start?* I thought to myself as I walked toward the cottage.

Everyone was up early the next morning eager to go out for breakfast and on to the beach. "Okay, let's go, the ocean is waiting for us." My wife smiled. We all jumped in the car and headed off for waffles and waves. We stopped at the local diner for breakfast and I noticed the ad for the local drive-in-theater posted near the register.

Playing this week
Jaws
Movies start at dusk
Bring the family

By the end of the afternoon we finally arrived back at the cottage, and I had time to set up my lawn chair, fix myself that icy gin and tonic, grab a paperback and settle down for a late afternoon libation. I would have been content to relax in my chair sipping gin and tonics every afternoon for the rest of the week; but the beach beckoned and my family would not be denied.

Returning from the beach on the third afternoon I spotted a billboard again advertising the Jaws movie at the drive-in. I was instantly inspired with a great idea. If I took the kids to see this movie about a great white shark terrorizing a beachfront community not unlike the one we were staying in, that just might curb their enthusiasm for swimming in the ocean. My diabolical mind couldn't have been more accurate. After going to the drive-in that night and watching the shark chew up swimmers in the mythical town of Amity, my kids were not in any hurry to return to the beach. Even my wife was concerned about the kids swimming in the ocean. I silently congratulated myself on the success of my fiendishly clever plan to get less time at the beach and more time for sipping gin and tonics in my lawn chair.

After a few more abbreviated visits to the beach, I spent all but one of the remaining late afternoons slouched in that lawn chair sipping gin and tonics, reading the paperback books I'd brought along, and admiring the sun glimmering off the waters of Cape Cod Bay. On

Friday, the last full day of our vacation, that one rainy afternoon that always happened during a Cape Cod vacation arrived. We spent most of the afternoon exploring the shops and boutiques in Provincetown. My kids were most impressed by one of the residents clad only in white painter's coveralls strolling down the sidewalk with a parrot perched on his shoulder. The bird had a colorfully lewd vocabulary which he used in loudly cursing everyone who walked past.

Saturday morning we packed up the car and headed back home. As I drove west on the Mass. Pike I had no idea that I was an alcoholic and that in the next few years my disease would rob me, and my family, of a whole lot more than just a few days at the beach.

EASTER BUNNIES

Gene and I were having a few drinks and discussing what my wife and I were planning for Easter Sunday. Gene dated my mother-in-law and was a good friend of our family, so of course I told him that he was invited for Easter Sunday dinner.

My kids no longer believed in the Easter bunny, but we still lined their Easter baskets with cellophane grass and filled them with marshmallow yellow peeps, chocolate bunnies and peanut butter and chocolate eggs. It was as I was telling Gene all this that he suggested, "Even if the kids don't believe in the Easter Bunny, I bet they'd enjoy having a couple of real rabbits to play with on Easter." Knowing what rabbits are noted for doing, I immediately began to squelch the idea.

"I don't want rabbits screwing all over the house in front of my kids. It's not a good idea, Gene."

"I'll make sure they're the same sex so you won't have to worry about that." Gene reassured me. Getting assurances from Gene was akin to a promise that everything that he sold out of the trunk of his car was completely legit, and hadn't "fallen off the back of a truck in New Jersey."

After a few more drinks, having two little furry bunnies around for my daughter and son to enjoy seemed like a great idea. "Okay. I'll bring them over late Saturday night. I bet the kids will just love them." Gene smiled.

Late that Saturday night, as promised, Gene showed up with the rabbits. Oh! They were so furry and cute we knew that the kids wouldn't be able to resist them. On Easter Sunday morning as the kids were searching for their Easter Baskets we took the bunnies from the closet where we had hidden them and brought them out to the surprise and delight of our children. They each scooped up one of the rabbits and began petting their soft fur. As they were trying to decide what to name them, they put their new furry friends down.

The rabbits began hopping around the house, exploring their new surroundings. It was only a matter of minutes before they started dropping tiny pellets of rabbit shit on the living room rug. I gave Gene a sarcastic smile. "Well, I guess that's what rabbits do!" He laughed. At the moment his laughter started to subside the rabbits started doing something else that rabbits are noted for. One of them mounted the other and began humping like mad, all the while one of his rear legs beating a staccato rhythm on the floor.

I yelled at Gene, "Well, there's something else that rabbits do!" I thought they were going to be the same sex"

"It's hard to tell." He replied weakly.

The kids had settled on names for the rabbits as I was trying to think of a way to get rid of them. This wasn't going to be easy. Who in their right mind would want two fornicating defecating bunnies running around their house? Nobody, that's who! As we sat at the table eating Easter Dinner, I was contemplating ways to euthanize the rabbits without breaking my kids' hearts. As I gouged out the clove eye of the butter Pascal lamb, I decided to put thinking of a solution on the back-burner until the next day.

Early Monday morning I was at the office telling my coworkers about the Easter bunny dilemma at my house. They thought that rabbits screwing and shitting all over my house was hilarious. I told them that they wouldn't think it was so funny if the bunnies were humping and dumping all over their houses. Then good old Lou came to my rescue. "I'll be happy to take them," he said to my amazement.

"Why would you want them after what I've been telling you?"

Being of Italian ancestry Lou replied, "Have you ever tasted Coniglio in Potaccio? It's rabbit seasoned with garlic and rosemary." I winced as I thought of Flopsy and Mopsy (or whatever the kids had named them) being sautéed in wine, butter, garlic and rosemary. "It's delicious, their meat is quite tender." Lou was in a gourmet's rapture as he continued to describe, in detail how the dish was prepared. I cut him off saying that I was grateful that he was taking the rabbits off my hands, and like Pontius Pilate I wanted to wash my hands of the entire episode.

I went home that night and tried to explain to my children as delicately as I could that we just couldn't keep the bunnies. "They wouldn't be happy being inside our house all the time. Lou had a nice farm where they could run and play outside all day," I lied. They were a bit teary-eyed at losing their newly acquired pets but reluctantly agreed that the rabbits would be happier at Lou's.

Just another alcohol fueled idea that hadn't worked out too well. I didn't give it much thought then. Even now, almost 40 years later, every once in a while my son will mention the Easter bunnies. I don't know if he believes how truly sorry I am about the bunnies, and a lot of other things I did and failed to do as a father. But I am!

BOOZE IN THE GROCERIES

Keeping up the illusion that we aren't drinking that much isn't really much of a challenge for us alkies. I had a small but well stocked liquor cabinet in the dining room. It was the closed door portion of a side board that also contained a wine rack. I always had quarts or fifths (before the liquor industry went metric, just to confuse us) of scotch, gin, brandy, rum and a few other potables. Once in a while my wife would make one of those snide comments that drunks really hate. "Don't you think you're drinking too much?" she'd ask, adding, "I noticed that you've been making quite a dent in that scotch in our liquor cabinet." *Where did she get off calling it "our liquor cabinet?" She hardly drinks anything at all,* I murmured to myself. *And is she marking the damn bottles?*

Avoiding any future inquiries about my alcohol consumption (at least out of the liquor cabinet) was a no-brainer. Whenever the level in any of the bottles was dropping enough so she'd notice, I'd head out to the supermarket to get a few items that we didn't really need. I'd place the bag on the front seat of the car and make a beeline for the package store. Once I bought a pint of whatever liquor was getting low, it was back to the car where I would hide the booze in the bag (it was easy, the bags were all paper back then) of the unnecessary food items. Upon arriving home I would simply wait until my wife was upstairs, or otherwise preoccupied, quickly add the contents from the pint into the matching brand, and then quickly bury the empty bottle in the wastebasket.

And then there was sneaking drinks out of those same bottles. This usually occurred around 2 or 3 a.m. when I returned home from a night of drinking at any of the local bars. I would quietly unlock and open the front door, and navigate, or stumble my way, to the dining room. Once I'd made it to the liquor cabinet, I'd pull out a bottle and head into the kitchen, get a rocks-glass out of the cabinet and pull an ice-cube-tray out of the freezer. "Shh" I slurred to myself. "Mustn't wake anybody up ," as I slid the ice-cubes slowly down the side of the glass. The clinking of the ice cubes was only a few decibels lower than the noise I'd made bumping into and or knocking over the furniture. Nothing wrong with having one more drink, even if gulping alone in the dark sitting on the floor in the kitchen. Is there?

STEAK IN A CAB

In my early thirties I entertained lofty political ambitions. I had run for, and was elected a Town Meeting Member. I figured I would be outstanding as one of the representatives of my precinct and that I would soon be campaigning for office at the state level (not unusual for an alcoholic to have such grandiose thoughts). After a year as a Town Meeting member, I was nominated by the governor to serve as his representative on my town's Council on Aging, fueling my ambitions for greater political glory.

All four members of the Council were invited to attend a symposium on elderly issues and concerns at the state capitol. We could also bring our wives along with us. The symposium would end around five and we could spend the evening having dinner at any one of the numerous restaurants in the city followed by an evening seated in the Governor's box as we watched our American league baseball team play a home game.

And so, on a gorgeous spring afternoon, my wife and I began the two hour drive to the state capitol. We arrived at the hotel and met with the other members of the council and their wives for a quick drink at the bar. We all agreed to meet at the bar again later and hire a caravan of cabs to take us to the restaurant that we had chosen for an early dinner, and then on to the ballpark.

Polishing the mahogany in the hotel bar wasn't a problem for me. Despite my wife urging me to "Take it easy," I was two or three scotches up on everyone else by the time we got into the cabs and headed for one of the best steakhouses in the city. The eight of us were seated at a table covered with white linen and while the others were perusing their menus, I was preoccupied with the Carte des Vins. I was a good cook, and selecting the best wine to accompany a gourmet meal and tasting a bit of it while I created culinary delights in the kitchen was the cook's privilege. Perhaps sensing that I might make an issue of it, the others at the table deferred to my expertise and allowed me to pick out the wine.

When the sommelier arrived and proceeded with the ritual of

opening the wine, presenting the cork, and offering me a taste of the Freemark Abby, California Cabernet Sauvignon that I had selected, I was uncoordinated enough to knock over my scotch as I made room for the wine. This produced a bit of nervous laughter from a few of my fellow dinner guests. Being a sensitive alcoholic, I overreacted with a loud, indignant, and slightly slurred, "I ordered you fuckin' people one of the best red wines from California and, that's how you show your appreciation. Well you can all enjoy your dinner without me. Go to hell." My wife was purple with embarrassment and the other guests at the table sat in astonished silence as I put my steak into a doggy bag and stormed out of the restaurant.

I jumped into a cab that was parked at the curb in front of the eatery and muttered the name of our hotel to the driver. As he navigated the city streets, I pulled the steak half way out of the doggy bag and began to gnaw and tear at it like a hungry dog. As I continued to attack my medium-rare treat, at some point I glanced up to see a look of disbelief and the wide eyed stare of the cab driver reflected in the rear-view mirror. When we arrived at the hotel, I lurched out of the cab, paid the driver, staggered through the lobby and somehow found the elevators, got off on the correct floor and found my way to our room.

I never got to sit in the governor's box and enjoy that ball game. It took months of apologies and promises before my wife would even entertain the idea of going anywhere in my company. And, I'll bet that there is a retired cab driver in the state capital that is probably still telling his grandchildren of the night he had a drunken idiot chewing on a steak out of a doggy bag in the backseat of his cab.

OVERNIGHT GUESTS

In the late '60s I tended bar part-time at a roadhouse that featured a great rib-eye steak special, fabulous pizzas, and go-go dancers gyrating on a stage behind the horseshoe-shaped bar. Curiously, Thursday nights were just as popular as Fridays and Saturdays. Part of the reason for Thursday's popularity might have been that the go-go dancers who would perform all weekend would start on Thursday night.

The bar had a policy of pouring the booze into a mixed drink last. The owner's reason being that the drink would taste stronger and the customer would think that we had been overly generous in pouring. The amount of liquor we poured into any drink was not up to the bartenders. Affixed to the tops of all the bottles were chrome attachments that metered out exactly one ounce, no more, no less.

I worked three nights a week, Thursdays, Fridays and Saturdays. After working there for several weeks, I noticed another way that the owner was keeping his overhead down by deceiving the customers. Behind the bar there were three shelves that held all of the bottles we poured from and also formed the outside edge of the island where the girls danced in their gilded cage. The top shelves were at waist level and held the most called for brands of whiskey. Side by side on that top shelf were the Seagram's VO and Canadian Club. While pouring those two brands I could see that their labels were soiled and a bit worn. On the bottom shelf (at floor level) stood the less frequently ordered liquors. Along with those less popular quart bottles was a ½ gallon of McNaughton's Canadian Whiskey, a brand I'd never heard of and one that none of my customers had ever ordered. Suspecting that the McNaughton's was being used to fill the VO and CC bottles I began to take note of the level of whiskey in that bottom shelf half gallon. It didn't take long to confirm my suspicions. They were substituting the cheaper brand for the VO and CC .

While the owner was deceiving his customers, the other bartender and the waitress he was screwing were screwing the owner, only it wasn't a threesome. At the end of every evening the owner would buy the staff a drink. As we sat at the bar enjoying our drinks on the house the bartender's waitress/girlfriend would order a pizza to go from the kitchen. Shortly before we left, she would go into the kitchen and come out with the pizza and place it on the bar. This time she perched the box on the bar so that part of the box hung over the edge. Someone bumped into the pizza box and it fell to the floor and flipped open revealing three rib-eye steaks. The owner immediately fired them both.

A few of us thirstier employees would usually head for an after-hours ginmill in the next town down the road. We were often accompanied by the go-go dancers who had nowhere else to go except to their hotel room. On this particular night, after a few rounds, the two go-go girls drove down to their hotel which was just a block down the street. They returned about 10 minutes later crying that somebody had screwed up and that they didn't have a reservation at the hotel and that there were no rooms available. "Donn'tyuu worry about a thhhing you can shleep at my house." I slurred. They were delighted. So was I.

I drove the five miles to my apartment (I should say our apart-ment, my wife's and mine) in record time. When we pulled in I could see that the lights were still on. *Oh, well, she won't mind,* I thought. Wrong! She sure did mind. She was out on the porch before we got to the front door. She glared at the two girls. "Where do you two think you're going?" As drunk as I was I knew that the question didn't need an answer. The girls knew too; they ran to their car and were gone. Then she turned to me. "What were you thinking? That it would be okay to bring two women home with you?" I feebly replied, "Well, they didn't have a hotel room, and I told them that we have a sofa-sleeper." I wasn't slurring my words anymore. She just rolled her eyes, and said, "I'm sure you'll be comfortable on the couch tonight."

THE COP AND THE LOBSTERS

Paul the chef/owner of the seafood restaurant where I tended bar, was a heavy hitter. Weekends were the busiest and in the sweltering heat of the cook-run he would often consume a fifth of brandy and the lion's share of a case of Budweiser while putting out hundreds of dinners. When the rush was finally over, he would come out to the bar exhausted, sweating profusely and ready to relax with "the regulars" who had congregated to have a few. They would always stay 'til closing, and occasionally Paul would tell me to lock the doors and he would loudly announce that from that point on, "Drinks are on the house!" This was met by cheers from the regulars and sighs from myself and the other bartender, knowing that it was going to be an even later evening for both of us.

One of those after-hours drinking fests lasted quite a bit longer than usual. I found myself sharing one more for the road with Paul at around five in the a.m. "Christ, my wife is going to be pissed at me when I get home." I moaned. "Oh, don't worry about it." Paul smiled. "Tell her we were taking inventory, and just grab a couple of lobsters out of the tank and surprise her with a seafood brunch." We both agreed that taking inventory was a great excuse and that the lobster-based brunch was an absolutely brilliant idea.

As Paul was getting ready to lock up, I a grabbed a shallow cardboard flat (the kind a case of beer in cans comes in) out of the back cooler and pulled a couple of lobsters out of the tank in the dining room. We said good night, or more accurately good morning out in the parking lot and I placed the lobsters on the back seat of my Volkswagen Beetle.

The crustaceans and I were in the last five miles of the 12 mile trip home when I spotted the blue lights of a police cruiser in my rear view mirror. I pulled over and a local police officer strutted up to my side window, flashlight in hand. It was barely dawn and he shone the flashlight light into my face as he asked for my license and registration. As I fumbled in the glove compartment for the registration, he directed the beam from his flashlight into the back seat. He jumped back and yelled, "What the hell is that," as the flashlight illuminated the two lobsters crawling around in their cardboard corral. "Oh, they're a surprise breakfast for my wife." I mumbled. "I'm really late getting home and we figured that if I brought her some lobsters we could have a nice brunch and she wouldn't be too pissed at me," I explained.

He smiled; well, maybe it was really a sneer. "Well, I'm a little pissed at you for driving on my highway in this condition. If I catch you again your ass is grass and I'm the lawnmower. You and your lobsters take it slow for the rest of the way home."

Inebriated driving encounters with law enforcement were not taken as seriously back in the '60s and '70s as they are today, and rightfully so. If you're convicted of a DUI in my home state these days, it's an automatic loss of license and when you add up court costs, fines and surcharges by the insurance company it comes to a hefty sum. I recently spotted a billboard that pictured a red-eyed young man taking a breathalyzer test. The copy read: "Congratulations, you just blew $10,000." The billboard was on the side of the same highway where I was stopped with the lobsters.

THE HOLIDAYS

Many A.A. groups celebrate members sobriety anniversaries collectively at the end of each month. December usually has the smallest number of celebrants. That's because for us alcoholics the holidays is the one time of year when our drinking a bit too much doesn't stick out like a sore thumb, because so many others are getting into the "Holiday Spirit!" Or, in our case, "spirits."

For me it would begin about two weeks before Christmas. In the 1970s I worked for one of the largest companies in corporate America. It was located about 15 miles south of my home. The Vermont state line was 10 miles north of home. Vermont had, and still has state-run Vermont Liquor Stores. When I started to prepare my annual list of holiday refreshments that I was absolutely going to need, I wouldn't dream of not letting my co-workers take advantage of the much lower prices offered by the Green Mountain State. So I would offer to pick up their booze for the holiday season when I drove to Vermont to pick up mine. On the day before my liquor run, I'd go from cubicle to cubicle picking up everyone's money and their lists of whatever they wanted for the holidays.

For several years I drove a red Volkswagen Beetle. It was totally dependable for winter driving in New England, so I never had to worry what the weather or road conditions would be like when I made my run to Vermont. Hell I'd have gone no matter what nature had dished out. *"I was on a mission from God,"* I thought.

As I eased my VW into one of the parking spaces in front of the state liquor store, my joy knew no bounds. I glided through the front doors, pulled out the list, tapped the wad of cash in my pocket, grabbed a shopping cart, and was off to the races. First stop gin, let's see: three fifths of Tanqueray, two Beefeaters, one Gordon's and now on to the scotches: two Chivas Regals, one Johnny Walker Red and one Black, three J&Bs and one Dewars. And so it went, through the vodkas, rums, tequilas, brandies and an assortment of cordials. I was plucking those bottles off the shelves faster than a fiddler's elbow. By the time I got to the checkout I looked like Nicholas Cage in the opening scene of **Leaving Las Vegas**. Even though all that liquor wasn't mine, though a good portion of it was, I was thrilled just to have temporary custody. The dozens of bottles would clink softly inside their bags and cartons as I drove off. I had this image of myself: I was like Santa, only I was bringing booze in a red VW instead of toys and presents in a sleigh. Who the hell thinks like that?

Then there were the obligatory visits to relatives and friends. I didn't need to make a list of which ones to drop in on. The aunts and uncles, cousins, friends and neighbors who doled out plenty of "holiday cheer" were easy to remember.

I'm going to interrupt myself here. I didn't know how I was going to end this, but fate, it seems, has lent a hand.

Two days ago on December 23rd I had an appointment with a Clinical Dietitian in conjunction with a significant weight loss associated with my diagnosis of Pulmonary Fibrosis. As the young woman outlined a plan to help me gain weight, she asked one of the routine questions that was part of the intake procedure. "Do you drink alcohol?"

"No" I said.

"Not any at all?"

"No not for 36 years." I answered.

"May I ask you a personal question?"

"No, I don't mind at all."

"Are you a member of Alcoholics Anonymous?" She waited

"Yes, I am."

Upon hearing my reply her eyes filled with tears. She reached across her desk and clasped my hand. "My mother up in New Jersey just celebrated two years of sobriety. Thank God for you people!"

Alcoholics in the throes of their disease have a horrible ripple effect on those they love and almost everyone they come in contact with. With alcoholics in recovery the total opposite is true. Sometimes I forget that.

$5,000.00

Getting indicted by a grand jury was a shocker. Myself, along with the three other members of the local state agency, were accused of violating the public trust and failing to adhere to bidding statutes when awarding contracts to numerous vendors who provided goods and services to the agency.

After recovering from the initial blow of reading the indictment, I sat wondering what to do next. My grandiose plans for a political career had flown out the window when the summons was delivered to the front door. I sat at my kitchen table drinking scotch and thinking that I would probably (probably really!) need a lawyer. At that very moment came another knock at the door. It wasn't a deputy sheriff with another summons, but our close family friend Gene, the very same Gene who had suggested the rabbits as an Easter surprise for my kids.

Gene's appearance was less than impressive: his wardrobe looked like it had been retrieved from a dumpster, his haircut a black and gray palm tree hit by hurricane force winds, his horn-rimmed eye glasses held together at the left corner by a piece of duct tape hung lopsided on his nose. He also lived a radically different lifestyle than we did. He had for the most part an apartment devoid of furniture, with a refrigerator that contained nothing more than an onion and a jar of mustard. His car was a beat up old Dodge sedan, the floor of which was ankle deep in empty beer cans and fast food wrappers. The trunk, however, was always filled with merchandise that varied according to what had recently "fallen off" of a truck in New Jersey, like bootlegged 8-track tapes, jewelry that turned your skin green, Chanel No. 5 that was made in a Brooklyn bathtub, cartons of cigarettes smuggled up from the Carolinas, booze, and every summer, fireworks in time for the 4th of July.

I couldn't have had a better source for referring me to legal counsel. After reviewing my indictment, Gene gave me the name of the best criminal defense lawyer in the county. He also told me that he would demand an upfront $5,000.00 retainer. *Where the hell was I going to get five grand?* I thought. Gene must have read my mind or the dazed look on my face. "Don't worry kid." He reassured me. He then proceeded to lay out $5,000.00 in one-hundred dollar bills on the kitchen table. "Here, take this and don't worry, you can pay me back when you can."

I hired the high powered attorney that Gene had recommended. It took almost a year before the case came up in trial court and when it did my lawyer advised seeking a plea bargain rather than going to trial. I took his advice and ended up with a suspended sentence and one year's probation. During the following two years, I had joined A.A., stayed sober and continued to pay Gene whatever I could afford, as often as I could manage. I had the balance that I owed down to around $800.00. In all that time Gene had never said a word to me about what I called "My kitchen table loan." I had made a few extra dollars that month so I was able to pay Gene back $500.00 instead of the usual two or three hundred. "Hopefully I'll be able to pay off the balance next month." I said as I handed him the cash. "That's fine, I'm glad I was able to help you out," Gene replied.

Gene died unexpectedly the following week. I was deeply saddened by his sudden passing. He had been a family friend for many years and would be missed by all of us. Gene was always there when I needed him and was there when I had needed him most. But, to be totally honest, for one brief moment a selfish thought did creep into my mind, *Why couldn't he have died last week and saved me $500.00?* So much for being a grateful recovering alcoholic!

A NIGHT AT THE MOVIES

My son was 8 and my daughter 12 years old when I got sober. Prior to that time, their mother often did not, because of my drinking, leave them in my care for long periods of time. Occasionally she would venture out to a movie with one or more of her girlfriends. When she did I could drink the way I wanted.

I had a system worked out that would allow me to have as many drinks as I pleased during the two or three hours that she would be gone, and with my alcoholic logic, not allow my kids to witness or interfere with my drinking. Let's assume that the movie would begin at 7 p.m. Within 10 minutes after my wife left the house, I would come up with an excuse as to why the kids had to go to bed early. Often these movie outings would occur on a Friday evening. To overcome the children's protests about such an early bedtime I would tell them that we would be going on a special trip to the mall or an exciting adventure at the zoo the next day and we would have to get started early in the morning. These promised excursions seldom, if ever materialized. After a time the broken promises no longer worked, so I had to resort to that old parental response to their arguments as to why they had to go to bed: "Because I said so, that's why!" On several Saturday mornings my wife would be dealing with two disappointed kids and a hung-over husband. Despite her protestations and pleadings, I repeated these actions on several occasions. She finally stopped going to the movies altogether.

What never occurred to me was the obvious danger that I put my life and the lives of my children in. If, God forbid (how many times did I invoke the name of the Almighty?) there was a fire, how could I rescue my children or save myself if I was blacked out on the couch? The obvious question here is: how could you, time after time, endanger the well-being, the very lives of your children?

There is a paragraph on page 24 of the book Alcoholics Anonymous that offers an insight as to why.

"The fact is that most alcoholics, for reasons yet obscure, have lost the power of choice in drink. Our so called will power becomes

practically nonexistent. We are unable, at certain times, to bring into our consciousness with sufficient force the memory of the suffering or the humiliation of even a week or a month ago. We are without defense against the first drink."

A COW IN THE WINDOW

You ever have that uneasy feeling that someone is watching you?

I had a part-time job tending bar (a lot of alcoholics do) at a small seafood restaurant about thirty-five miles from home. It was set in a hollow at the intersection of two county roads in a rural location. Business was brisk on weekends; the dining room would turn out a hundred dinners or so. During the week you'd be lucky to turn out a dozen meals, but we had a great group of regulars who sat at the bar and kept me busy. There was an old jukebox in one corner stocked with mostly country and western tunes that rarely got any money put into it except when someone who was passing through would drop in a few coins.

It was a half-past 2 a.m. when one of those customers passing through who had been quietly sipping rum cokes ambled over to the jukebox, dropped in some change and punched up a sad lament about losing the one you love. It played three consecutive times. On the first spin of the 45 he mumbled the words along with the record, by the second time he was wiping tears from his eyes, and on the third play he was sobbing uncontrollably. The regulars tried to console him, but he just paid his tab and was still crying loudly as he stumbled out the door. "Poor bastard, wonder what made him break down like that?" one of the regulars wondered, "Well gentlemen, it's just about that time; last call," I announced. I had a Chivas Regal along with my customers as they drank up and speculated as to what the rum and coke drinking stranger had been so broken up about.

After my regulars had departed, I locked the door, poured another scotch and began the closing routine. First thing was always the money: count out the register, run the tape, and balance the total. Put all of the cash in a bank deposit bag and hide it in the freezer, underneath the boxes of U15 shrimp. Refill my scotch then clean up behind the bar: restock the beer refrigerators, make sure there were full bottles in the speed wells, wash the last few glasses, wipe off the bar, and empty the remaining goldfish crackers out of the bowls on the bar and back into their large square waxed container. Normally I would have one or two drinks while closing up, but as is often the case with alcoholics, once we begin to drink we can never predict how many we will have. I may have had as many as seven or eight scotches on this particular night. One more quick one as I drained out the sinks, shut off the lights, locked up and left for the forty minute drive home at 3 a.m. On this particular night it would take me a lot longer than forty minutes to make it home.

The route home would take me through several small towns and over several miles of back-roads. On one point on that rural byway the road forks; to get home, I would bear to the right; on this drunken drive home, I went left instead. In an alcohol induced blackout I drove my car through a barbed-wire fence into a cow pasture. I came to in a fuzzy alcohol induced haze, I could hear birds chirping, and it had to be five or six in the morning. As my eyes slowly opened to a squint, I could tell that it was a gray overcast sky. The feeling that I was being watched swept over me and as I turned my head toward the driver's side window, I was face to face with a large eye peering through the open window of my Mustang. The eye belonged to a large black and white Holstein cow who was probably just as surprised to see me in her pasture as I was to wake up there. As I sat upright in the driver's seat, she backed away from the car and returned to her grazing.

"How did I get here, and where is here?" I asked myself. I turned my car around and drove back through the hole I'd made in the barbed wire fence that enclosed the pasture. I spent the remainder of the time driving home trying to come up with an excuse for being out all night that my wife would believe. The fabrication might fly, but how was I going to explain the barbed wire scratches on the hood and sides of the car?

WINE STEWARD

Working as a wine steward at a five-star restaurant is a hell of a deal for a functioning alcoholic. The restaurant was so high end that my title was Sommelier, which is French for wine steward. Being somewhat of a gourmet cook at home, I had selected a lot of "appropriate wines" for the elegant dinners that I prepared. I made a big deal of soaking the labels off of the bottles, pasting them in a binder and recording my impressions of the particular vintage that I had selected and served. Sounds pretty elegant, doesn't it? In fact, I was a lot closer to drinking out of a paper bag than I realized.

The package store where I often bought my wines was operated by the brother of the five-star restaurant owner and he mentioned that his brother was thinking about hiring a wine steward so I should give him a call. He gave me the number and I called that same day. The following day I was at the restaurant being interviewed. I was offered the position on the spot and I accepted immediately. My heart was pounding as I left. I was going to be a Sommelier, wearing a silver tastevin (originally called a *tasse à vin*) hanging around my neck on a chain and serving select vintage wines and champagnes to sophisticated clientele. Oh, I looked resplendent in my dark blue vest, napkin folded on my forearm, tastevin swinging on its chain and my folding combination corkscrew and knife peeking out of my vest pocket. Since my job also involved selecting most of the wines, the corkscrew and lots of samples for yours truly were provided by the salesmen who sold wines to the restaurant. It was a dream job for an alcoholic. I was getting free bottles of wine to try and sipping wines (professionally mind you) two or three nights a week. I even attended a wine tasting event in Boston that had French bread flown in that morning on a Concorde jet from Paris.

On Valentine's Day 1979 I had been asked to conduct a wine tasting seminar at the restaurant for a class of culinary arts students from the local community college. It went exceedingly well; they were fascinated as I expounded on vintages, and went from identifying the Premiers Crus of the Gironde to telling them the somewhat exaggerated story that Dom Perignon, a Benedictine monk had discovered champagne and called out, "Come quickly, I am drinking the stars." The event went so well that I invited the waiter who had been assigned to help out and was returning to college in Boston the next day to go to a nearby café and have a couple of drinks to celebrate the success of the wine tasting. We didn't stop at a couple (I rarely did) and I vaguely remember being asked to leave by the owner.

After dropping off my assistant I headed home. I had promised my wife that I would prepare us a nice dinner that evening. It was late afternoon, I was drunk and about 15 miles from home when I plowed my Buick into a snow bank. The two city cops who arrived to check out the accident must have been very impressed with me. Here I was staggering around the car in my three piece suit, briefcase in hand, and my left arm still in a cast from arriving home drunk and falling down the stairs onto my flagstone entryway three weeks earlier. Somehow they took pity on me and just put me into protective custody instead of charging me with a DWI.

After spending a few hours in a holding cell I called my brother-in-law to come and pick me up. As I waited for him to arrive my hung-over brain was feverishly trying to come up with something to say to my wife that would convince her that, once again, I was really sorry this time. She'd heard all of my excuses too many times before, so as I sat silently in my brother-in-law's passenger seat, I came up with what I thought would get me off the hook. I'd tell her that I thought I might have a problem with alcohol and that I would call Alcoholics Anonymous. Maybe that wouldn't be enough, so I figured I'd add the dramatic gesture of emptying out my liquor cabinet and offering the contents to my brother-in-law. He didn't drink much so I figured he'd decline the offer.

When we got to my house my wife was waiting at the door. I quickly told her about my possibly having a problem with alcohol and that I would call A.A. She was still plenty mad but readily agreed that I might have a problem with booze. Then came the gesture that I was convinced would be declined. I offered the contents of my liquor cabinet to my brother-in-law. He accepted; I couldn't believe it. I put all of the bottles into a cardboard box; tears streamed down my face as

I handed it to him. They were real tears, not the alligator ones I always produced when begging for forgiveness yet again.

In A. A. parlance, the phone call that I was to make to Alcoholics Anonymous the next day would be the end of "What it was like" and lead to what's known as "What happened."

WHAT HAPPENED

What follows in the second part of the trilogy describes my arrival and early experiences in Alcoholics Anonymous. It chronicles the changes that occurred in me and some of the people and events that enabled them to happen. In my first year as a member of A. A. I had much to learn about how to stay sober.

At the meeting celebrating my first year of sobriety a longtime member affectionately known as "Sneaker George" pulled me aside, and said two things to me. "I was watching you when you came in here, Kid; I knew you weren't convinced that you were an alcoholic. I was convinced that you were and I hoped you'd stick around long enough to figure that out." He then said something truly prophetic. "You keep coming here, you won't believe how good it gets."

THE LIST, THE CALL,
THE MEETING

On the morning of February 15, 1979, the day after my Valentine's Day debacle, my wife presented me with a three-page handwritten list (by no means a complete one) highlighting some of the things I had done and failed to do in my drinking career and how she felt about them. I had heard the litany hundreds of times before. But somehow seeing them in black and white made them impossible to ignore. Those three pages were probably the most sincere and honest love letter that I have ever received. One item glared at me: "For all the sleepless nights I have spent feeling lonely, hurt and worried because you were out drinking. For all the terrible days I had to drag myself to work after those sleepless nights."

As I had promised on Valentine's Day, I made the call to A. A. My fingers twitched as I dialed the Alcoholics Anonymous number. I didn't know if my call would be answered by a religious fanatic, eyes glazed with that look of saving mankind for God, or a teetotaler preaching the evils of demon rum. It was neither; it was an answering service that assured me in a recorded voice that if I left my number, someone would return my call. *Great*, I thought, *I hope no one calls back*. I had only promised to make the call. Thirty minutes later the phone rang. A calm, reassuring and familiar sounding voice quietly suggested going to a meeting and not drinking for just one day. He said *they* would pick me up at 7:30.

The voice on the phone knocked on my door promptly at 7:30, as promised. I was surprised and amazed to see Richard looking back at me. I had worked in his store when I was a high school student. He smiled and said, "Come on, we'll take you to a meeting and you can see what you think." He introduced me to two other guys sitting in his car. I jumped into the back seat of the Chevy station wagon and we were on our way to my first Alcoholics Anonymous meeting.

As we walked into that church basement there were handshakes, greetings and words of welcome along with the offer of a freshly brewed cup of coffee. I tried to avoid eye contact with anyone as I got my coffee and sat inconspicuously in a folding chair in the very last row. I didn't want to see anyone and I sure as hell didn't want anyone to see me. I was only 34 years old, and here I was in a church basement full of old drunks. *I don't belong here. This is the worst moment of my life,* I thought.

As the meeting began I noticed the hands of the people seated in my row. Thick weather-beaten digits that had banged downed countless draft beers at local taverns were now wrapped around fragile white Styrofoam cups of coffee. Delicate fingers that had sipped too much wine from Waterford crystal lay folded and relaxed. I tapped my coffee cup, and etched lines into the soft Styrofoam with my fingernails.

I didn't remember too much of what was said at that first meeting. I was too busy thinking of reasons why I didn't belong in a room full of alcoholics, but my mind kept going back to the hands, mine too shaky to stop moving or hiding, theirs calm and steady. It was their hands that made the difference. They held on when I could not, they gripped me in the fellowship of Alcoholics Anonymous. They grasped me with a firmness of conviction that came from having been where I now was, steeped in the denial that whatever was wrong couldn't possibly have anything to do with my drinking.

Immediately preceding the forward in Pass it On, the story of Bill Wilson and how the A.A. message reached the world, which is published by A.A. World Services Inc., there is an excerpt from a letter sent to the General Service office:

"I'll never forget the first time I met Bill Wilson. I was a couple of months sober and so excited to actually meet the co-founder that I gushed all over him with what my sobriety meant to me and my undying gratitude for his starting A.A. When I ran down, he took my hand in his and said simply, 'Pass it on.'"

What I would come to learn is that those guys in that Chevy station wagon were doing exactly that.

EPIPHANY

It's defined as a sudden intuitive understanding, but mine was so subtle that I didn't even know that it had happened. It wasn't a dramatic white light or burning bush experience that other members of A. A. spoke about. Despite keeping the wine steward job (minus the tasting cup) I had been staying sober and going to meetings for a few weeks when it happened.

I usually finished up at the restaurant right after the dinner rush and be on my way home by 9. Contrary to the advice I'd gotten from A. A. members about not going to bars, I stopped at one of my old watering holes. I made my way to the bar and ordered a club soda. The crowd was already well on their way to wherever they were going, and there I was standing with my club soda and feeling sorry for myself. I wasn't drinking and didn't really belong there and I didn't feel like I belonged in A. A. either. It sure as hell wasn't *Cheers* and nobody wanted to know my name. They say that when one door closes, another opens. I was in the hallway and it was a bitch. All they did in A. A. was tell me to shut up and listen. They already knew how to drink and that was all I had to offer. I needed to learn how to stay sober and they would tell me how to do that. I took another sip of my club soda and left.

It was the next morning when I realized that when leaving that bar I had subconsciously made a decision to stick with Alcoholics Anonymous and see what would happen. I would take their suggestions, get a sponsor, use the list of phone numbers that they had given me to call other sober alcoholics.

They had also told me to "stick with the winners." I wouldn't have recognized a winner if he hit me over the head with a 2x4. I knew that I was a winner. People used to call me a winner all the time. They'd roll their eyes, use that disgusted tone and say "Boy, you're really a friggin' winner." I don't think that that's what those A. A.s had in mind.

I would follow all of their suggestions, and when they didn't work, and I drank again, it would be their fault, not mine. I reluctantly decided to take the advice that Richard had given me after that very first meeting. "You will find these basics especially helpful in early sobriety: don't go to places that serve alcohol, don't hang around with people who drink, and don't keep booze in your house." I resigned from the wine stewarding job, dropped out of touch with most of my friends who were mostly drinking buddies anyway. I made an exception with the third item. I reasoned that my modest wine rack made from old wood and metal milk crates and stocked with two or three dozen bottles under the cellar stairs was out of sight so that would be an allowable exception.

I didn't mention the wine in the cellar to anyone, least of all my sponsors. On Halloween of that October that decision would come back to haunt me (I couldn't resist) and almost be my undoing.

THE CUT MAN AND
THE STREET DRUNK

When I had newly arrived in Alcoholics Anonymous, they spoke of miracles that had occurred in the lives of those who got sober. How they had completely turned around and become useful and well respected members of the community. Miracles were nice to hear about in theory, but I wanted more tangible proof of what they were telling me. Then I met David and Jack. Both were members of the W.O.R.M.S. an acronym that stood for: We Only Ride Motorcycles Sober.

David rode a big orange BMW that we called the "Great Pumpkin." He kept it on the front porch of the rooming house where he lived. He had arrived in Alcoholics Anonymous several years before I did. Back then he rode a Harley Chopper and was a "cut man" for an outlaw motorcycle gang. His job was to physically punish people who had incurred the gang's wrath for whatever reason. He preferred to use a knife for that purpose, and by his own admission he did it with a sadistic relish.

During his years of sobriety David had put away his gang leathers and traded in his Harley for a dirt bike which he raced with consummate skill, even winning a state title for Enduro racing.

More importantly, David had returned to college and received a degree in Molecular Biology which he put to use working as a researcher at the Memorial Sloane Kettering Cancer Institute in New York before returning to Massachusetts.

Jack had also arrived several years before I showed up. They told me that when he showed up at A.A. he was living in the streets and all he owned were the pitiful rags on his back. He shook so violently that he couldn't even hold on to a cup of coffee except by using both hands and they would only give him half a cup at a time so he wouldn't spill it.

By this time Jack was riding a Vespa, had a rented room and a few changes of clothes, but he was no slave to fashion. His teeth were a dull brown from the tobacco that he constantly chewed. His uncombed hair contributed to his slovenly appearance. But Jack was a genius when it came to the relatively new and expanding world of computers.

He had graduated with a double major and was recruited by some heavyweight companies the day he left campus. Among them was The Carabinieri (The Italian National Police). Jack had been flown to Rome where he designed and installed all of their sophisticated software.

These guys weren't theoretical miracles or legends to be bragged about; they were real and I could and did have coffee with them. We would go on motorcycle rides together and they would tell me what they had done in order for these miracles to occur in their lives. They were tangible evidence that convinced this doubter that miracles did happen in A.A. and that they could even happen in my life as well.

NURSE NANCY

She had arrived wearing a brand new fall coat which she hung on the back of her chair. She was in fact chairing the A.A. meeting being held in an empty factory building. Just before the meeting started with the usual moment of silence, Francis came in and sat in the empty chair right next to Nancy. Francis was an old street drunk who blew into his old hometown about once a year. He had a predictable routine. Francis would hit up the local rectories and parsonages and cajole what monies he could out of the local clergy that would buy him some more beer or wine, his two beverages of choice.

Francis must have scored a few bucks on that day because right after the Serenity Prayer that immediately followed the moment of silence, he produced a warm can of beer from the pocket of his overcoat, popped the top and sprayed beer foam all over Nancy's brand new coat. Whatever amount of serenity the prayer had managed to give Nancy immediately abandoned her. "Francis, you dumb son-of-a-bitch!" She screamed. "You've ruined my brand new coat with your goddamned beer!" Francis just responded with one of those nonplussed *what-the-fuck-just-happened* looks.

Most of the people attending the meeting either stifled a laugh or expressed concern either for Francis or Nancy's coat. I had only been coming around for about three weeks and was shocked to see someone actually open and drink a beer right at an A.A. meeting. The old guy next to me said he'd known Francis for years and wasn't surprised in the least.

Francis had another clever little angle that he used to raise funds to fuel his addiction. He would walk the downtown streets and throw himself into the side of a slow moving car, fall to the pavement and feign injury and con the driver into giving him a few bucks so he wouldn't have to report the incident. Many years later Francis would miscalculate, and instead of bouncing off the side of a woman's car he ended up dead under the front wheels.

I had been wrestling with a problem when I showed up at the meeting that night, I had largely forgotten about it after the beer spraying incident but Nancy, in spite of her coat being sprayed, had noticed my agitation and reluctance to stick up my hand and ask for help. She approached me after the meeting had ended. "You know we're not mind readers. We can't help you if you don't ask us to." So I explained that I was concerned about an ongoing issue with a coworker. Nancy offered some sound advice that involved working one of A.A.'s 12 steps to address the problem. It was not the last time she would come through for me. Many years later I was faced with a far more serious situation and Nancy would once again provide me with an invaluable perspective that would serve me well on many occasions.

It was eleven years later when I was 45 years old, my manager told me that the corporate giant I worked for was going to sell our division and we would all be out of a job. He didn't know exactly when it would happen but probably within a year or so. I was devastated. My plan was to take an early retirement at 55. By that time I'd have 30 years with the company and I'd get a great golden parachute or whatever they gave you when you retired. So I went to a few meetings and whined about it until Nancy showed up one night.

Once again she took me aside after the meeting, sat me down at a table, took out a pen and a large sheet of paper. On it she drew a large circle in the middle and lines extending out in all directions from the edge of the circle. At the end of each line she drew a smaller circle. "Okay, here you are," she wrote my name in the middle of the large circle. "Now these smaller circles represent all of the things that you are. Let's fill them in." She began writing: father, son, brother, husband, artist, A.A. member, neighbor, friend. When she had finished filling in all of the circles, she made her point. "You see, you are all of these things. But like most humans when something is wrong with any one of these parts of us, we tend to give it more importance than it deserves. Yes, it should be looked at, addressed and considered, but remember that it is part of who you are, not everything that you are."

"Kind of like a new fall coat is just a small part of what and who you are." I reminded her.

She smiled, gave me a wink and a hug and whisked out the door.

I would use that illustration many times in my personal life over the years and pass it on whenever I thought it would be helpful.

Nurse Nancy went on to host a controversial call-in show on the local public access TV station. She was an ardent feminist and received a lot of hateful calls filled with misogynistic invectives which, due to a non five second broadcast delay made it on to the air.

She married the show's producer, some guy with a Teutonic name like Thorman or Thurman. Together they co-wrote and produced a one-woman show that toured colleges and universities across the USA to rave reviews and standing room only crowds.

SPONSORS

Getting a sponsor is a vitally important part of the A.A. program. It is highly recommended that you select a member who has accumulated some length of time in recovery, so that he or she can guide you through A.A.'s 12 Steps of Recovery. When I saw those 12 steps displayed on the wall at my first meeting I figured I was in real trouble; there were only 10 commandments and I hadn't done too well with those.

Selecting a sponsor was really a no-brainer for me. I had known Richard since I was a teenager working in his store after school and he had responded to my call to Alcoholics Anonymous, and also taken me to my first meeting. During the second or third week of going to meetings in the backseat of that Chevy station wagon we stopped to pick up Joel. The first thing I noticed when we walked in was his Harley Davidson shovel-head standing right there in the kitchen. Joel was a no-nonsense down-to-earth bearded biker and I figured he would be just the kind of guy who wouldn't pull any punches and have a hard-nosed approach to the A.A. program. Boy, was I ever right!

Richard was also a motorcyclist but of a different description. He kept his BMW in the garage and his form of sponsorship, although no less effective, wasn't quite as blunt as Joel's. Having been a motorcycle rider in high school (I had to sell my bike when I got married at 21 to buy a refrigerator) was also a factor in picking my two sponsors. Richard was very persuasive in getting me to use those 12 steps that I mentioned earlier. When I would go to him with my latest problem or crises in my newly sober life he would ask, since he knew that I wasn't applying any of them, "Well, what step are you working?" That was his way of guiding me toward using the steps. He always called them the meat and potatoes of the program.

Both Richard and Joel were charter members of that group they called the W.O.R.M.S. (We Only Ride Motorcycles Sober), that I described in "The Cut Man and the Street Drunk." The group was composed of about 30 or so other members of A.A. They got together for rides to out-of-town meetings and every September went down to the Shenandoah Valley in Virginia to an A.A. regional convention. Mid-winter they would gather to plan rides for spring and summer and share a pot-luck-supper at Richard's spacious and historical (a revolutionary war captain's) colonial home.

I hadn't owned a motorcycle for several years and wanted to join, since I didn't have a motorcycle, I felt that I couldn't become a member. Citing the first step of Alcoholics Anonymous that says, "The only requirement for A.A. membership is a desire to stop drinking," they reassured me that I could indeed become a member: "The only requirement for membership in the W.O.R.M.S. is a desire to own a motorcycle." I joined up immediately. It would be a year later that I would again own a motorcycle and go on those rides. It wasn't until years later that I would realize what an important part of my sobriety my membership in the W.O.R.M.S. really was.

I was program chairman for an A.A. group and one of my duties was to get a speaker for the Tuesday night meeting. I had met Fred from East Arlington, Vermont fairly early on in my sobriety. He was an A.A. legend. He not only knew A.A. co-founder Bill Wilson, but had accompanied him on 12th step calls. When pressed on the fact that he had known Wilson, Fred would always smile and say, "Here, shake the hand that shook the hand." I called Fred and asked if he would speak at a Tuesday night meeting for me. "Sure, I'd be happy to. When do you want me?" We picked out a Tuesday that was convenient for him and I couldn't wait to tell the group who I had gotten for a speaker. Although I had known Fred for several years, I had never heard him tell his story. I was sure that he would dazzle us with stories of Bill Wilson and the early days in Alcoholics Anonymous, pearls of wisdom cascading down on the audience as Fred passed on the very essence of A.A.

The Tuesday night arrived, the meeting was S.R.O. (Standing Room Only), I introduced Fred, sat down and heard him say, "When I came around the most important thing they told me was to get a hobby, preferably one that didn't include drinking." He waited for the laughter to subside. My jaw dropped as he said; "I bought and started to ride a motorcycle."

GOD IS IN THE COFFEEPOT
AND I AM THE TREASURER

I hadn't been around A.A. too long when both of my sponsors suggested I get an A.A. job. The purpose of getting a job in Alcoholics Anonymous was so that I would become involved with a group and become a member, making it my home group. There were several service positions available at the various meetings that I regularly attended: program chairman, setting up chairs, brewing coffee, sweeping up after meetings, and washing out cups (which back then included emptying and wiping out ashtrays). I had quit smoking two years before and wasn't keen on cleaning ashtrays. The step meeting that I attended on Wednesday night needed a coffee maker, so the following week I volunteered.

Making coffee each week demanded that I show up early and begin filling the large urn. There was this one guy who showed up early every Wednesday. Billy G. would ride in on his BMW and sit on the counter while I made coffee and chat with me about everything from motorcycles, to A.A., to transcendental meditation. The meditation came up when we were discussing the 10th step which states that we can improve our conscious contact with God through prayer and meditation. "I've got an example of putting the 10th step into practice," says Billy, "Well, I wanted to give this meditation thing a serious try so I hiked up a nearby mountain and sat on a ledge overlooking a secluded forest glade. Just when I was starting to feel the calm and serene benefits to be derived from meditating there in nature, a young couple romps into the glade, spreads out a blanket and does a little meditating of their own. In the missionary position!" I'm laughing hysterically, and Billy is too.

Humorous meditation story aside, I learned lot about A.A. and life from our conversations in that kitchen with Billy G. Volunteering for that coffee job allowed me to absorb a lot of A.A. wisdom, one on one from Billy and several others who just happened to show up early on a regular basis.

There is an old guy in Vermont who says at the end of every

meeting. "God is in the coffeepot, thanks for helping Him out." But thanks to guys like Billy G., I know who was really helping who.

I had been making coffee for about three months and managed to miss the monthly business meeting. Here's a hint for newcomers; don't ever do that! When I returned the following week they informed me that I had been elected group treasurer and would be responsible to gather up all of the donations made each week and deposit the money into the group's checking account. Alcoholics Anonymous has no dues or fees of any kind; monies collected at meetings go to support the group by buying items like coffee, A.A. literature, cleaning supplies. My immediate response was, "You can't make me your treasurer. I am just not a trustworthy person. Why, I was indicted by a grand-jury. I'm barred from holding public office in the Commonwealth for life." As they handed me the checkbook and the cash, they said, "That don't matter here kid, you'll be all right."

I went home that evening and found an old vintage tobacco tin to put the money in until there was enough to make a deposit. I stuck the tin in a compartment of the roll-top-desk. Tears came to my eyes as I did so. These people had trusted me with a key to the church, cash and a checkbook. I was barely certain that I could trust myself; they had to know that I wasn't very trustworthy either. Yet they had trusted me. And because they had trusted me, in that very instant I became trustworthy.

My kids were teenagers at this time and when they became adults they confessed to being a little less trustworthy than their father had been. One evening over dinner they somehow brought up the subject of the "tobacco tin" in the roll top desk. It had been many years since I'd been treasurer of the group and a longtime had passed since the tobacco tin had held any bills or coins. They both smiled that impish smile that siblings have when they've put something over on Mom or Dad. "Well, you know whenever we needed money for a six-pack we would often raid that tin box. Usually you'd let it build up to $70 or $80 before you made a deposit and we figured you wouldn't miss a couple of bucks." A.A. money being used by teenagers to buy beer. A little ironical, wouldn't you say?

THE STEP DEBATE

It was at a Wednesday night meeting that it happened. I couldn't have been more than a few months sober. It was a step meeting. The usual procedure was to select the particular step to be read and discussed on that particular evening. On this night we were delving into

Step 10: Continued to take personal inventory and when we were wrong promptly admitted it.

The group was following the normal format of reading a paragraph or so and then stopping to discuss what had just been read. They were in the middle of the paragraph that speaks of "justifiable anger" when the conversation took an unexpected hard left turn. A relative newcomer raised his hand and commented on how he'd found the 10th step helpful in his early recovery. One of the group's long time members (a bit of a bleeding deacon) shot his hand up as stiff as a Nazi salute. "You're only a few days sober and you're telling us about the 10th step?," he bellowed. "These 12 steps were placed in the book in order and that's the way you have to take them." Across the large table that dominated the small room in the rectory where the meeting was being held, another hand went up just as quickly as the previous one had. Another long timer (this one more of an elder statesman) said, "First of all, there is no such thing as *have to* in Alcoholics Anonymous."

Hands were going up all over the room, each person ready to weigh in on the issue. The chairman could hardly call on people soon enough. When the dust settled, the meeting was roughly divided into two groups; one that was firmly convinced that the steps were written in order and that was the way they should be worked. The other group was adamant that the steps should be viewed as a tool box, from which you could select the best one for whatever the situation demanded.

"Are you telling us that this is a pick-what-you-choose step recovery buffet?" challenged one of the in-order supporters.

"You're missing the point!" yelled a dissenter from across the room.

And so it went back and forth. The chairman had all but given up trying to keep some semblance of order as the meeting descended into utter chaos. Finally the debate was ended when a little lady from Alaska (not Sarah Palin) quietly and with finality said, "The only way to work these steps wrong is with a drink in your hand." The debate was over!

RICHARD

Richard was my first A.A. sponsor. Not a very flowery introduction to a man who literally saved my life. He would have wanted it that way. I first met Richard when I was a high school student and went to work in his retail store for a couple of hours each day after school and all day on Saturdays. My job mostly consisted of sweeping the floors, cutting up a never-ending supply of cardboard boxes that needed to be taken to the dump, stocking shelves, and to my delight, doing the window and interior displays, which I seemed to have a natural flair for and that Richard encouraged.

The store did business on two levels. As you walked in off the street on to the main floor there were ladies fashions. Everything from dresses, slacks, blouses and pocketbooks to kerchiefs, bras and panties. At the rear of the store was a narrow stairway that led to Richard's office, an elevated perch with an open view of the sales floor below. A wide shelf which ran the entire length of the opening that looked out over the sales floor served as his desk. The desk was always cluttered with what seemed like reams of notes, bills, orders, ad copy, and invoices. There was an old massive iron adding machine whose worn buttons Richard's fingers would dance over with amazing speed. An old coffee mug filled with pencils and pens was adorned with a logo so faded that you could no longer read what it had once advertised. Right next to that coffee mug sat a slightly faded red tomato pin cushion stuck with dozens of straight pins, T pins, hat pins and even an open safety pin or two. And, an ever present crossword puzzle book.

Downstairs on the basement floor were the household goods. Venetian blinds, curtain rods, window curtains, sheets and pillow cases, throw rugs, drapery and dress goods, and a small display of kitchen gadgets: can openers, vegetable peelers, measuring spoons and even mousetraps.

Most of my hours at the store were spent outside the back door of the lower level cutting up that endless supply of cardboard and stuffing it into the back of Richard's station wagon and driving it to the dump.

I worked at Richard's store for three years as a teenager. I had no idea that the man I admired so much for being so smart and successful as a business man would be even smarter and more successful at saving lives, including my own. Richard was the man who showed up at my door to take me to my first meeting when I made that reluctant call to Alcoholics Anonymous.

When it was suggested that I get a sponsor early on in A.A. I immediately went to Richard and asked him to take on that role. He smiled and reassured me that he would be happy to accept the responsibility. I must have climbed that narrow stairway to his elevated office at the rear of his store with a multitude of problems large and small thousands of times over the years. He almost always had time to step out for a quick coffee at the small restaurant just down the street. If not, he'd roll back his office chair, prop his feet up and take the time to listen to my latest problem or tale of woe. He never failed, not once in 32 years, to guide me through my current crisis with patience, wisdom, and understanding. Richard had trained as a navigator on a B-17 during World War II. He always knew where he was going, and lucky for me, he took me along too.

Richard had a rapier sharp wit and a dry sense of humor that never failed to delight and impress me, even when it was at my expense. Throughout the length of my sobriety we would meet almost every day for coffee at a local family-owned restaurant. Our conversations ranged from motorcycling adventures to local politics and of course A.A. Often we would end up humorously taking the inventories of our fellow members. On one particular morning Richard reminded me, "You have to remember that most of the people in A.A, aren't wrapped too tight. You and I are all right. But, I'm not too sure about you!"

A few days before Richard would close the store and retire, we sat at that long shelf desk of his. As he placed a few personal effects into a cardboard box, I pointed to the tomato pin cushion. "Can I have that as a souvenir?" I asked. "I don't even know why I want it. Maybe because it's prickly like your personality." I smiled. He smiled back as he handed it to me. It still occupies a place of honor on my desk.

As befitting a veteran, Richard died on November, 11, 2011. He was still my A.A. sponsor. I was at an A.A. meeting in Charleston, South Carolina when I got the call that he had passed. I know he would have liked that.

JOEL

There are sponsors who exude so much sweet love you could pour it on a pancake. Joel is more that tough love kind of guy, not the syrupy variety. I asked Joel to be my second sponsor, calculating that my chances of staying sober would double with two sponsors. I also figured that anybody who parked his Harley in his kitchen would be capable of providing me with some of that tough love.

Within a week of asking him to sponsor me I found myself walking out of a meeting with Joel. "Boy, that was a lousy meeting." I complained.

"I don't ever want to hear you say that again," he barked. "If you don't like what's going on at a meeting, stick your hand up and change it, otherwise just shut up and listen."

I never offered that criticism again. *Well, this what you asked for,* I told myself. It would not be the only time that what Joel had to say would cause the hairs on the back of my neck to bristle.

I was at a Dunkin' Donuts having a coffee with Joel on a sunlit Saturday morning when I began taking the inventory of a mutual A.A. acquaintance. Joel stopped me mid-sentence: "You know Kid, maybe it's a good thing for you to be taking other people's inventories. Some day you might even have enough courage to take your own!" More of that straight to the point, no-nonsense tough love stuff again. As much as I resented hearing those barbed criticisms, I knew that they were spot on and that I needed to pay attention to them.

Joel had very definite opinions on everything to do with recovery in A.A. One action in particular incurred his wrath. Many times people would get up and leave a meeting to go outside for a cigarette or just to take a break from the meeting. Joel would often challenge them by saying, "You get sober by attending meetings, not hanging out in the 'half-measures availed us nothing' parking lot!"

Joel got so good at spotting my character defects that he could, in fact, read my mind. We were seated next to each other attending a speaker meeting in Vermont one night. I wasn't saying a word, shaking my head or making gestures of any kind; but just thinking to myself,

When is this guy ever going to find a point and make it? Joel leans over, smiles and whispers to me. "You need to be nice!" After the meeting I asked him how he knew that I was less than impressed with the speaker.

"Oh, your attention wasn't on the speaker but seemed to be wandering all around the room. Let me explain something to you, Kid. Whenever anyone has the courage to get up in front of a room and tell their story, they deserve our undivided attention. Try to remember that it's not just stories about a drinking lifestyle; we're talking life and death here."

The fourth and fifth steps of the program of Alcoholics Anonymous are often referred to as the action steps:

Step Four: "Made a searching and fearless moral inventory of ourselves."

Step Five: "Admitted to God, to ourselves, and to another human being the exact nature of our wrongs."

By mid summer of my first year of sobriety, I was ready to proceed on both of them. I had decided to trust Joel for his guidance in taking me thorough them both. He strongly suggested that I take that moral inventory in writing. It would be more thorough and less deniable if it were written. I spent days working on it. It was far from fearless; it was terrifying to confront myself with all of those serious character defects that I had managed to avoid looking at for my entire life. Joel reassured me that once we got to the fifth step, those defects would all become excess baggage that I wouldn't have to carry around anymore.

The day finally arrived when I was ready to share everything I had written with Joel. Trusting another person with all my sins, if you will, was not the same as going to confession to a priest. Joel wasn't bound by any vows of the confessional. Hell, there wasn't even going to be a darkened confessional booth in a church; we had decided to take a motorcycle ride to a scenic overlook and enjoy the view of the distant mountains while I owned up to every wrong that I could remember having committed.

It was an agonizing two hours, but I must admit the sense of relief at having completed the task was truly liberating. Bringing all of those things to a conscious level and then saying them out loud somehow put them in their proper perspective. Joel pointed out that many of the things that I had agonized about for years were simply not that important and could now see the difference in what I owned and what I didn't own. "We alcoholics usually think one of two ways: either everything is our fault, or nothing is our fault. Now you can see the difference. Quite a relief eh?" Joel then shared a couple of stories from his life as an active alcoholic. What they did was to relieve me of that terminal uniqueness that many alcoholics suffer from. "Come on Kid, you did a good job, now let's get out of here." Joel laughed as he started up his Harley.

"Wait a second; I'm going to burn my fourth step inventory list first."

MY FIRST 12TH STEP CALL

The twelfth step of Alcoholics Anonymous tells us that we should carry the message. It was midsummer in my first year of sobriety when I got the phone call from Alan, an A.A. member with 10 years sobriety, asking me if I could accompany him on a twelfth step call. "Of course, of course," I eagerly replied. *Oh my God, I'm going on my first twelfth step call,* I almost said out loud. Alan continued, "We're going to take this guy to detox; I'll pick you up in about 10 or 15 minutes. This guy lives right in your neighborhood, so you might even know him."

Alan arrived as promised and we were off to this guy's apartment. It was on the ground floor of a large old house that had been converted into four or five apartments. It was located on a busy street that was zoned residential and commercial so there were a lot of vehicles and pedestrians going by. We walked up the long sidewalk leading to his front door.

Carlos Castaneda was a controversial and popular author in the sixties. One of the theories espoused in his books was that places possessed an inherent power for good or evil. Walking into that apartment would have made anyone a believer of that theory. The evil was so palpable you could taste it. In the living room, the couch and all of the stuffed chairs had been slashed with a knife. The floor in the kitchen was littered with pieces of smashed and broken dishes and dirt from potted plants that had been thrown against the walls. In the bedroom, Carl, the subject of our twelfth step call, sat on the bed shaking, and obviously quite a bit under the influence, clad only in his underwear among piles of clothing that had also been slashed with knives. He was crying and pleading for help.

I stood there stunned by what I had just walked into when I heard Alan ask me to find a pair of pants and a shirt that hadn't been cut up so we could get this guy dressed and on his way to detox. I found a tee-shirt and an old pair of khakis on the floor of the closet, along with a pair of flip-flops. We managed to get the shirt and pants on Carl. Alan threw a pair of underwear and a toothbrush into a paper bag, and we were on our way. We walked out the front door. Carl was a bit wobbly so each of us held onto one of his arms to keep him from falling. As we walked down the long sidewalk heading for Alan's van parked at the curb, Carl started screaming that we were kidnapping him and for someone to call the police. Passersby looked on curious and concerned. I was mortified. "What do we do now?" I asked Alan. "Throw him in the van!" he commanded. We hustled him into the backseat of the van and we were off on the 15 mile ride to the detoxification unit at the local treatment center.

We were only two or three miles into the trip and Carl had already alternated between sobbing and uttering regrets and screaming obscenities at us and trying to throw himself out of the van. Alan had had enough. He pulled over to the side of the road, and told Carl to get out of the van. As we drove away I said, "We can't just leave him there on the side of the road like that. He's a danger to himself and maybe even to others. Maybe we should at least let the police know that he's out here?" I nervously suggested.

"Look he just wasn't ready yet." Alan responded. "We passed a State Police barracks a couple of miles back. I'll stop and you can go in and tell them. Okay?"

We did stop and when I told the desk sergeant about Carl being out there by the side of the road in a drunken condition his response was, "Well thanks for reporting it to us, but we can't do anything unless he does something first." When I got back to the car and told Alan, he just smiled. I was so nervous and upset that when we got back to town I asked Alan to drop me off at a meeting. My sponsor Joel was at the meeting and after I told him what had happened, he made me feel even worse. "You know that now, you're responsible for anything that happens to that guy."

I awoke the next morning to a photo on the front page of the local newspaper showing Carl being put into an ambulance. The story underneath the picture had Carl claiming that we had thrown out him of the van at 50 miles an hour. I was horrified. I called my other sponsor Richard and told him what had happened on my first 12th step call. And what Joel had said to me at the meeting I went to afterward. He told me not to worry about any charges coming from what Carl had told the police, and reminded me that although A.A.'s founder Bill Wilson had said;

**"Whenever anyone, anywhere reaches out,
I want the hand of A.A. to be there."**

"Just remember that sometimes, you get the finger in return," he added.

THE POPE'S BLESSING

I had quit drinking in February of 1979; it was early September and the Pope was coming to Boston. I had managed to get a few photographs published in the local newspapers during those few months and was excited when one of the editors suggested I go to Boston and try to get some photos of Pope John Paul II.

I clutched my Canon A-1 camera tightly as I stood in front of the Peace Garden at St. Leonard's Church in Boston's North End waiting for the Pope's motorcade. I was sure that the Pontiff would stop here on this narrow street when he spied the children with their yellow and white banner of welcome and the devoted parishioners carrying bouquets of yellow and white flowers. The children, the parishioners, and I smiled in anticipation as his motorcade slowly approached. I began focusing and clicking off frames as fast as I could. This aspiring photojournalist was going to get a great close-up photograph of the Pope when his open limo stopped in front of the church.

There he was: Pope John Paul II was right in front of me, and as the crowd in this predominately Italian neighborhood began chanting, "Viva Il Papa! Viva Il Papa!" he began blessing them. I let my camera hang from the strap around my neck as I reached into a pocket on my camera bag for another roll of film. When I did, my fingers brushed against the forgotten tiny sterling-silver Creed crucifix that I had bought and shoved into my camera bag while doing a photo essay on yard sales a few weeks earlier. For the moment I forgot about reloading my camera and brought out the crucifix. I strained against the muscular arm of the Boston police officer who was holding back the crowd. He glanced at what I held in my hand and gave me an approving nod as I thrust it toward the Pontiff. As the Pope's head turned, he paused, squinted at the tiny crucifix that I held out no more than an arm's length away. He smiled and blessed both the medal and me. The cars and motorcycles inched forward and we all waved as the taillights twinkled and the motorcade moved on. I dashed through Government Center toward Boston Common where the Pope would be celebrating Mass after his motorized tour in Boston ended.

The sunny autumn afternoon gave way to overcast skies, and as the Papal Mass commenced so did the rain. As the thousands who were attending the Mass opened their umbrellas, the rain began to transform the ground to mud. As the faithful knelt on the soggy earth for the benediction, they lit candles. The light from their candles did not illuminate much beyond their faces as they huddled beneath their umbrellas against the elements.

I left Boston that day with a few tight shots of the pope waving from his open limo in that narrow North End street and a few long shots taken on Boston Common. But something happened to me when Pope John Paul II squinted at me and gave me his Pontifical blessing. What I saw and felt in that fleeting moment was the simple faith and true spirituality that this man personified.

Since my arrival in Alcoholics Anonymous in February of that year, I had been working diligently on the 12 steps of recovery with my two sponsors. Both they and I were, in general, pleased with the progress that I had made to that point. But at some level I still struggled with part of Step 3 that asks me to turn my will and my life over to God as I understand him. I had spent half of my adult life as "self-will run riot" and was extremely reluctant to turn control of it over to anyone or anything. But on my way home from Boston I realized that for whatever reason, the powers that be saw that this alcoholic was struggling. They sent the biggest gun they had to personally help me!

THE WINE CELLAR

Early on in my sobriety I mentioned that I was advised not to keep any booze in my house. I complied with that advice, sort of. I had this small collection (a couple dozen bottles) of vintage wines stowed beneath my cellar stairs in old wood and metal milk cases. I figured that wine wasn't technically booze, and it was out of sight, therefore out of mind, hidden under the cellar stairs. It was now October 1979 and I'd been sober for eight months and had rarely given my "wine cellar" any thought at all.

It was Halloween week and my wife and I had argued over ordering a pasta maker as a Christmas gift for her Uncle Carmine. Why I would argue over a pasta maker is still unclear to me, but I had. She had stormed out of the house in a huff and I was upstairs taking a shower. I seem to have great ideas, insights and revelations while standing under running water. And I'd just had another one. *She's all pissed off about this pasta maker; I'll give her something to be pissed off about. I'll just march right down to the cellar and grab a couple bottles of Cabernet Sauvignon. Let's see how she handles that!*

I jumped out of the shower, dried off, donned a pair of sweats and was downstairs going through the kitchen on my way to the cellar. We had a wall phone mounted right next to the cellar door. Instead of opening the cellar door, I picked up the phone. Knowing that it was his day off, I dialed Dave's home phone number.

If I would have had a third sponsor it would have been him. Dave managed a Kentucky Fried Chicken outlet; unfortunately for him, it was just down the street from where I worked at the time. He could count on me walking in just about every day during my lunch hour. I got lots of good advice on how to stay sober and he would put me to work out back washing dishes, breading chicken or making coleslaw. He got free labor and I got free help with working my A.A. program. *Quid pro quo.*

Well, I rattled on for several minutes about my stubborn, hot headed Italian wife and the pasta maker. Dave kept interjecting "uh huhs," and "I sees" until I finally ran down. At the end of my tirade he asked one simple question: "Well did you learn anything, asshole?" We both responded together, "Don't keep booze in your house!"

I got dressed, emptied out the wine cellar and drove the contents over to my father's house. Over the next few weeks I managed to give all of the bottles away to folks I knew could properly enjoy it.

JUST PASSING THROUGH

It was early morning on Thanksgiving Day; very early morning. I was up at the crack of dawn preparing the annual feast for my family. I had made the stuffing, was ready to baste the bird, peel the potatoes and dice the vegetables. All this without my usual bottle of wine nearby on the counter-top. I had reluctantly come to the rooms of Alcoholics Anonymous in February of that year and this was going to be my first sober Thanksgiving.

As I sautéed, chopped, peeled and diced, I began to think of how not one member of my family appreciated all of my culinary efforts. My kids, ages 8 and 12, didn't care anything about all the hard work that went into preparing the dinner that they would hurry through without so much as a thank you. My wife wasn't even out of bed yet and I had done all this work alone. My parents would be coming for dinner and my mother would, as she always did, tell everyone how her stuffing was so much better than mine. And my father, fussy to the extreme, would push the food around on his plate, take a few bites and complain that he just wasn't that hungry. I couldn't believe that I was doing all this work for these ingrates.

I called my sponsor Richard and asked if he could meet me for coffee at the local fast food restaurant that was the only business in town that was open on Thanksgiving.

Ten minutes later I was seated across the booth from him. He listened patiently as I droned on at great length and with dramatic embellishments about my ungrateful family members. Finally, I wound down. "What should I do about this?" I asked plaintively. "Shut up! Grow up! Go home and get through it!" he replied.

We had coffee nearly every morning for years. We talked about anything that happened to be on our minds, whether trivial or important, it didn't matter, it was the pleasure of his company that I enjoyed.

These days we often hear that we now have a softer, gentler A.A. I don't know if we do or not. All I do know is that my sponsor still practiced the same type of no-nonsense A.A. right up until his death in 2011.

I was at a meeting in South Carolina a few years ago and instead of asking if there were any visitors from out-of-town, they asked, "Is anyone passing through?" *We're all just passing through,* I thought. A. A. was here a long time before I showed up and it'll be here a long time after I'm gone. I'm just glad that it coincided with Richard's.

WHAT IT'S LIKE NOW

After reaching my first year of sobriety, I found that there was much work still to be done in terms of dealing with my character defects -- serious flawed core behaviors that not only inhibited my growth in Alcoholics Anonymous but threatened my very sobriety.

My continuing encounters and experiences with people in A.A. over the ensuing decades would guide me through life experiences enriching and fulfilling, and sustain me through those that were terrible and traumatic.

What follows in this final section are portraits of some of those people and descriptions of a few of the experiences that have left indelible impressions on me as I continued in my recovery.

SPONSORSHIP

I was about six months sober when, on a ride home from a meeting, Joel and Richard collectively asked me what I thought my objective as a member of Alcoholics Anonymous was. I thought for a moment before I answered. "To stay sober, lead a better life and try to work the twelve steps of A.A. to the best of my ability." Richard came back with a lightning fast retort and a smile. "That would be a great answer to put on a self appraisal form prior to an annual review; if they had such a thing in A.A. You're in training to help other alcoholics." "But when do I get to do that?" I asked. "Don't worry the time will come," they reassured me. It would be almost a year before anyone would ask me to be their sponsor.

It was a warm summer night and I had gone on a twelfth step call with another A.A. member. We arrived at Roy's house to find him sitting on his front steps clad in Bermuda shorts and sporting a green tee-shirt that said, "Kiss me I'm Irish." He was trying to stuff his clothes into a cardboard box. They were strewn all over the front lawn where they had been thrown by his wife. It was a pretty good bet that nobody was going to kiss him, no matter what nationality he was. Roy said that he had phoned his mother and she said that he could spend the night at her house. We dropped him off and told him that we would pick him up and take him to a morning meeting the next day. He was ready and waiting when we pulled up at 9 a.m.

After the meeting we went for coffees at Dunkin' Donuts. Roy seemed genuinely interested in A.A. and asked a lot of questions. As we answered them, I was hoping that our responses wouldn't dampen his enthusiasm. I recalled what I had often heard when it came to talking about Alcoholics Anonymous to a potential newcomer: "If they're ready; you can't say anything wrong. If they're not ready, you can't say anything right." It turned out that Roy was ready, he'd had enough. Over the next few weeks he attended meetings daily. While driving home from one of the meetings he asked me if I would be his sponsor. Although he no longer attends meetings very often (not recommended), Roy remains sober to this day.

Over the years I have sponsored many A.A. Members: some have stayed sober, others have not. I take no credit or blame in either case. I am powerless over my own alcoholism, and I sure as hell don't have power over anyone else's.

I believe that the gift of recovery is offered to everyone who seeks it. Staying sober is not a matter of luck, but I have found that the harder we work, the luckier we get!

THE SEVENTH SON

My father was the seventh son out of ten boys and seven girls born to my grandparents. He, like his siblings, went to work in a New England textile mill at the age of 14. He worked there until he retired at age 65. Later that same year he was diagnosed with Amyotrophic lateral sclerosis, (ALS) also known as Lou Gehrig's Disease. ALS would take a little over two years to kill him. It was terrible watching this disease slowly consume this man who had worked so hard to provide for his family. It was my fifth year of sobriety when he died, and I did not deal very well with the loss of my father.

I was angry at God, at the disease, and at the fact that my father did not live to enjoy a long and well-deserved retirement. During those two years there were many decisions to be made with regards to D.N.R. orders, health care proxy powers, living wills and what seemed like reams of paper work from the various doctors and medical facilities involved in my father's treatment. My mother relied on me to help her with these often emotionally difficult decisions. Rather than behave like a responsible and dutiful son, I resented the fact that she was so dependent on me. It seemed to me that both she and my sister never felt that I did enough or visited with my father enough to suit them. None of this true; all of it was imagined on my part.

Rather than share all of these intense negative feelings with my A.A. sponsors or at local meetings, I was going to out-of-town meetings and not telling anyone a damn thing. I was hiding out in Alcoholics Anonymous.

I was determined that I would not go out of this world counting ceiling tiles in a hospital room and harboring a lot of melodramatic bullshit. In the meantime my anger festered to a point where I was behaving so miserably that my sponsor Richard decided to take some action; he wrote and mailed me a letter.

In the letter he took my inventory. When I read it I couldn't believe the things he said about me. He had written how selfish and uncaring I was in dealing with the disease of my father and the needs of my family during this horrible time. He went on at length on how I was failing to practice the principles of A.A. in my life. My initial reaction to his letter was not one of instant gratitude. " Who in the hell does he think he is writing that shit to me? I'll blow up his store with him in it." I said as I gripped the letter.

Billy G., the guy who always came early every time to that meeting where I was the coffeemaker, had told me that whenever I was emotionally upset over something I should wait 24 hours before taking any action or making a decision I might regret. I read Richard's letter again the next day and decided that I would just never speak to him again, which was a lot better than blowing up him and his store. I put the letter aside and read it again a few days later. On that third reading, I realized that someone had loved me enough to have the courage to take the time to tell me the truth about my behavior.

There is a thing about taking others inventories in A.A. You should never take anyone else's, just your own. I disagree. I was probably a lot closer to a drink than I realized, and had Richard not written me that letter, who knows? As for this alcoholic, there is nothing wrong with you taking my inventory as long as you do it with me, not about me.

THE PICKLE SLICER

A topic often discussed in Alcoholics Anonymous is the difference between an obsession and a compulsion as they apply to taking a drink. Here is a story that perfectly illustrates the difference.

An obsession is a state or feeling that completely occupies the mind. A compulsion is a force that makes us do something, such as acting on whatever our particular obsession may be.

John worked in the shipping department of a huge pickle factory. The shipping department was located way back at the rear of the building. In order for John to get to his workstation everyday, he had to come in through the front doors, punch his time card, and begin the long walk through the entire facility. First he would pass through the sizing room where the cucumbers were sorted and graded on a long conveyor belt. Next came the giant brine vats where the cucumbers were marinated and turned into the pickles themselves. The next area was the sorting room where it was determined whether the pickles would be sent out whole in jars, fed into the massive relish crusher, or over to the pickle slicer. Then came the packing area where the pickles, relish or slices were automatically packed into jars, labeled and ready to go to the shipping area to be placed in cardboard boxes.

But John suffered from an obsession; a strange obsession perhaps, but nonetheless he agonized over it every day. He couldn't even explain it to himself, let alone anyone else. John suffered from the obsession that for some reason he wanted to put his penis into the pickle slicer. For years he made the daily trek through the front doors, past the sizing conveyor, the giant brine vats, the sorting room, and the massive relish crusher. He would always hurry when he passed the pickle slicer lest he give in to his weird obsession.

The day finally came when John could fight the obsession no longer. After he had taken his usual route past the conveyor, the brine vats and the relish crusher, he came to the pickle slicer and his obsession became a compulsion, forcing him to act. He dropped his pants and put his penis into the pickle slicer. Just as he did so the foreman came around the corner. "What the hell do you think you're doing?"

he yelled. "I can't explain, pleaded John, "It's just a compulsion, I couldn't help myself."

"Well I can help you," cried the foreman, "You're fired. Now go clean out your desk and get out of here."

When John arrived home in the middle of the afternoon his wife was curious. "John, what are you doing home this early? Did something happen at work?" *How am I going to explain what I did to her?* he thought.

"Honey, I know you're going to find this weird and even hard to believe but I got fired today for putting my penis into the pickle slicer at work."

"You what? What were you thinking?" Her mouth hung open in disbelief.

"I've had an obsession about doing it for sometime now, and today it became a compulsion and I couldn't help myself. Just as I did it, the foreman came around the corner and fired me. He also told me that I had better get some kind of help."

"John, My God, into the pickle slicer. What were you thinking? What about you? Is your penis all right?"

"Yeah I'm fine." John answered. "What about the pickle slicer?" His wife asked. "Oh, they fired her, too."

9TH STEP PHOTO SHOOT

Whenever I'm at a step meeting and it's on the 9th Step, I'm tempted to relate this benefit from my practicing the 9th Step of Alcoholics Anonymous:

9. Made direct amends to such people wherever possible, except when to do so would injure them or others.

I ran into Sue, whom I'd treated poorly 20 years earlier, the "Wine in a Taxi" story. Well, here she is again, walking across a supermarket parking lot. "Well, hello, what a pleasant surprise!" She smiles. I notice that those big root-beer eyes haven't lost any of their mesmerizing sparkle. "Hi Sue, you look terrific. Tell me what you've been up to for the last 20 years."

"Well, I was married to a musician we're now divorced, I have two kids and live on a small farm just outside of town. How about you?"

I fill her in with the basics; "I'm married, two kids, a boy and a girl and doing some photojournalism as well as a bit of studio photography."

"Oh, don't be so modest. I see your photos published in the local papers quite often, and I was impressed with your one-man-show at the town hall last year. I have also admired some of your commercial work that I have seen." I blushed out a thank you.

I remembered that I certainly owed Sue an apology and an amend for the horrible way I'd treated her when we were dating. What better chance to practice Step 9 than here and now. I had thought of Sue when I initially did Steps 8 and 9 but had no idea where she was or how to contact her. *Okay, here goes,* I thought as I swallowed hard. "Sue, I've been a recovering alcoholic for going on five years now and part of my program consists of making apologies and amends to people I have hurt because of my actions. I know that at times I treated you shabbily to say the least when we were dating and I want you to know that I am truly and sincerely sorry for any pain I may have caused you." I stopped to breathe. She rolled her eyes. "Please know that for the most part you treated me very well. When you exhibited bad behaviors, which was mostly when you were drinking, I would remind myself that deep down I knew you were really a decent guy."

"Thank you for being so gracious in accepting my apology, and pointing out that our relationship wasn't all bad." What a relief it is to have you be so receptive."

"As for that amends part, I do have a request for you," she replied.

"What is it?" I asked.

"Well, even though I'm in my 30s now, almost everyone I know thinks that I still look pretty good. I exercise regularly and my body still looks like it did when we were dating." *Did she have to add that?* I thought. She continued, "Some of my girlfriends and I have been kidding around with the idea that I should submit a portfolio to *Playboy Magazine*. Would you be willing to shoot some nude pictures of me?" I realized I wasn't breathing.

"I'd be happy to do that for you Sue."

We set up an appointment for her to come to the studio the following week. She did indeed look as good as she had when we were dating, but I am proud to say that I conducted myself as a professional photographer, took the photos and collected a discounted fee that we had negotiated. Sue did submit the portfolio to *Playboy* but never made the centerfold.

Nonetheless, making amends to Sue a great convincer to me and to other alcoholics that there can be some surprising and amazing benefits to working the steps.

HAITI, AL-ANON AND
THE SWEATSHIRTS

It was the second of three trips I would make to Haiti. This time I was writing about and photographing a medical team from Vermont that was going into remote villages to assess and provide basic health care for the inhabitants. We were there for three weeks, and at the end of the first week, we went into the capitol city of Port-au-Prince to pick up more food and medical supplies, and to take showers since the mountain villages had no running water.

While we were in Port-au-Prince, I tried to locate an A.A. meeting. I tried the number listed in the tattered phone book at the Canadian Legation but the phone had been disconnected. I myself was feeling disconnected, not having been to an Alcoholics Anonymous meeting in almost two weeks.

When we returned to the mountains, the team settled into their routine of conducting clinics each day and then gathering in the early evenings to discuss and evaluate what they had observed during that day and lay out plans for the next. I noticed that a couple of the nurses were using familiar buzz phrases in their conversations that I often heard at A.A. meetings: "First Things First," "One day at a Time," "Easy Does It." *Hmm, maybe these women are A.A. members.* I thought, I waited until they were alone and asked if they were members of Alcoholics Anonymous. "Oh, no, we're very active in Al-Anon up in Vermont, one replied. I disclosed that I was an A.A. member and had been unsuccessful in trying to find a meeting when we were in Port-au-Prince. I then suggested that we could perhaps hold some kind of informal inter-group meeting of our own if they were so inclined. They were delighted with the idea. Each day for the next two weeks, we took an hour to sit on a rock beside a dusty footpath in the Haitian mountains and do our best to help each other cope with the hardships and horrible conditions we observed in that poor impoverished country.

Al-Anon sometimes gets a bad rap from some A.A. members, or is the object of good-natured ribbing. My wife became very active in Al-Anon shortly after I joined A. A., and she found their help in coping with my alcoholism, and my recovery, invaluable.

Many years had passed and I was asked to speak at an Al-Anon gratitude dinner by an A. A. member whose wife was very active in the local Al-Anon chapter. Remembering how helpful those Al-Anon nurses had been to me in Haiti and how my wife had praised Al-Anon, I of course said that I would be honored to speak to them. I had no idea of what to say to a group of Al-Anon members so I immediately called my sponsor Joel. I told him that I had committed to speak at an Al-Anon dinner and was unsure as to what to say. "Lie to them; they're used to it."

"That's awful. True, but awful." I shot back.

"Just kidding. They were a big help to my wife Mary when I first came into A. A. Mary went with me to my first A. A. Meeting. Hell, she looked so bad from living with me that they thought she was the alcoholic."

I did speak at that Al-Anon dinner and it was a delightful experience. All of the All-Anon members were warm and welcoming and were genuinely appreciative of my having come to speak to them.

Over the years my kid sister had also become active in Al-Anon. In Al-Anon they call us alcoholics "qualifiers" for their members. Her qualifier was her son who was into his own addiction at the time. I am happy to say that he has been in recovery for many years now, has a beautiful family and owns a very successful business.

During those many years as a member of Al-Anon, my sister attended an annual September retreat out on Cape Cod. One year she returned sporting a sweat shirt embroidered with an Al-Anon slogan which read "Unconditional Love" right over the heart in purple, green and gold thread. Hey, aren't those Mardi Gras colors?

The following month I was down in Florida attending an A. A. gratitude dinner. The guy at the front door was selling fifty-fifty raffle tickets. Half of the monies collected to one lucky winner. The other half helping to defray the expense of putting on the dinner. He was sporting an A. A. sweatshirt with an embroidered slogan that was a bit more in your face than its Al-Anon counterpart; "Shut up and Get in the Car," it read.

A. A. IN HEAVEN

There is proof that Alcoholics Anonymous exists in Heaven. A man arrived at the Pearly Gates and was greeted by St. Peter.

"Welcome to Heaven!" The man looked bewildered. "But, I don't belong here," he protested, "there must be some mistake."

"We don't make any mistakes here in Heaven." St. Peter replied. "If you're here it's because you deserve to be."

"But I've led a horrible life," the man continued. "I was a liar, a cheat, an alcoholic, a thief. I had the morals of an alley cat. How could I possibly qualify to be in Heaven?"

"Well, there are places here for many different types of people; we will just have to see where you fit in," St. Peter assured him. Into Heaven they went.

They were soon walking down a brightly lit corridor, with many large white doors on each side. St. Peter opened the first door. Inside people sat on rows of white benches staring straight ahead in silence. "Who are those people?" asked the newly arrived man. "Those are the Protestants," replied St. Peter. "I don't think I'd be too happy there," the man said. "Don't worry; there are many other places in Heaven let's continue on," said St. Peter.

They walked a ways further eventually arriving at yet another white door. Once again St. Peter opened the door; this time revealing another group of silent people. These men and women were kneeling in long rows of pews and repeatedly making the sign of the cross. "Who are those people?" the man inquired.

"Those are the Catholics, St. Peter answered.

"Well, I'm afraid I wouldn't be too happy being with them either. I'm starting to worry that I was so bad down on earth that I won't even be happy in Heaven."

"Don't despair; we will find just the place for you." St. Peter reassured him.

They came to the third big white door. (It's always the third one, isn't it?) St. Peter swung the door open. The smell of fresh brewed coffee wafted out and before they entered the room, the man could hear the sounds of pleasant conversations. When they went in, much to his delight, he saw small groups of men and women gathered together sharing that fresh coffee, munching on cookies and donuts, smiling pleasantly and warmly hugging each other. "Wow! I really like the looks of those people. Who are they?"

St. Peter gave him quizzical look "We don't know because they won't tell us. It's some sort of anonymity thing.

A MEETING IN QUEBEC

It was a gorgeous summer afternoon and I was riding my BMW motorcycle along the banks of the St. Lawrence River heading north. As the river began reflecting the afternoon sun, I decided to call it a day. I pulled into the small town of Saint-Gabriel looking for a campground and the possibility of catching an A.A. meeting. I wasn't having any luck finding either one. The gas station owner said that the nearest campground was quite a distance away, and my Eastern States A.A. Directory didn't list any local meetings. It was getting on toward early evening, so I decided to make finding a meeting my first priority; I could always check into a motel later. In my extensive travels I had realized that the cops always knew where A.A. meetings were, so I got to a pay-phone and dialed the local number for the Quebec Provincial Police. I told the dispatcher that I was a recovering alcoholic and that I was looking for a meeting in Saint-Gabriel or one nearby. She replied, "I don't know where any meetings are, but one of our policemen is one of those people; stay right there and I'll have him call you."

A few minutes later the pay-phone rang, "This is Sergeant Henri Perreault. I understand that you're looking for a meeting," he said with a heavy French accent.

"Yes," I responded, "I was trying to find a campground and didn't have any luck, so I'll need a motel room too. Can you recommend one to me?"

"I can help you out with both. I have a big backyard where you can pitch your tent and we can go to a meeting tonight at 7 o'clock. I'll drive by and you can follow me to my home."

Within a half-hour I had my tent set up in his backyard and was sitting down to a home cooked supper with him and his wife. We sat at the kitchen table talking about my French-Canadian heritage (my mother was born in Lachine, a part of greater Montreal), some of his experiences as a provincial policeman, motorcycle riding, and of course Alcoholics Anonymous.

It was coming up on 6:30 and Henri suggested that we'd better get going. "*Nous allons!*" he commanded. As we drove to the meeting

Henri said, "By the way, how is your French? It's a French speaking meeting." I told him that I spoke enough to get in trouble. He laughed and said, "I'll tell them to speak slowly."

We arrived at the church where the meeting was being held in the parish hall. I immediately noticed that all of the men were attired in crisp shirts and dress slacks. The women wore skirts and blouses or dresses. Seeing my look of astonishment, Henri said, "It's Friday night, and we always go out for pie and coffee at a local restaurant after the meeting." I protested, "But I'm wearing jeans and a tee-shirt." He reassured me that I'd be fine."

I did better than I thought I would in keeping up with what was being said at the meeting. When it came time to pass the basket for donations to support the group (there are no dues or fees in A.A.), they passed around a black velvet bag instead. All the alcoholic in me could think of was Crown Royal whiskey.

After the meeting everyone did get together at a rather upscale local bistro. Everyone ordered the blueberry pie which I guess was their signature dessert. We all exchanged handshakes and hugs in the parking lot as we bid each other *adieu*.

As I was taking down my tent on Saturday morning Henri came out into the yard. "Come on in; you can't leave without a nourishing breakfast under you belt." His wife had prepared a *tourtière* (a French Canadian meat pie). Since it was being served for breakfast, we drizzled a little maple syrup on top of our slices. They waved to me and as I drove out of their yard they called out "*à bientôt*" (see you soon). I am of the opinion that no one takes better care of its members than Alcoholics Anonymous does. These well-dressed French Canadians had proven it to me once again.

A CONSTELLATION OF MIRACLES

Back-to-back hurricanes were heading toward the home I had purchased in Florida. I was up in Massachusetts, and frenzied with of worry about the possible destruction of my winter residence in the Sunshine State. I knew that I had to, in A. A. Jargon, "Turn it over." I was trying all of the ways I'd been taught to do just that. Praying about it, talking over my concerns with my sponsors, sharing at meetings -- none of them were working. I had even attended Mass, received communion and offered it up, asking God to help me. I was even thinking about flying down to Florida. What was I going to do, hold the roof on with my bare hands when the hurricanes came barreling in?

If it were you with that problem, I could have resolved it for you in a heartbeat. Yet in spite of all my efforts, all the help and advice I'd been given, I couldn't let it go. I was sure people at meetings were sick of me whining about my problem and just wished that I'd shut up. I was at a Sunday morning meeting when I thought, *Oh, what the hell, I'll complain about the lack of a miracle in my situation one more time.* Just as I finished, one of the women who regularly attended the meeting shot her hand up.

Leslie had thrown herself out of a third floor window of a psychiatric facility where she was being treated and often shared things that were more than a little left of center. On this particular morning, though she was as right as rain. "As for miracles, most of us who have been around these rooms for any length of time and reflected on it could honestly say that their lives were *constellations of miracles.*" She wasn't looking right at me but her words hit me like a punch in the face. My God, that was my problem, pure and simple. I had lost sight of the multitude of miracles that had occurred in my life in the years that I had been sober, not to mention that being sober in itself was a miracle of the first magnitude.

Instead of being grateful, I was fixated on something that hadn't even happened and certain that the worst possible scenario would occur. I was impatient that, despite all of my efforts, results had not come immediately.

The twin hurricanes did hit the Florida town where my house was. Damage to some dwellings was minor; others were completely destroyed. The extent of damage done to my home was slight. The roof of my car-port had been slightly buckled and a couple of shutters ripped from the side of the house by the high winds. In the end, this experience would became another addition to my personal constellation of miracles.

A. A. AT WALMART

In case you might have the impression that I might qualify as the poster boy for Alcoholics Anonymous, the following will convince you that I do not.

It was five or six years ago on a visit to the local Walmart Super Center. I was in need of only two items: hair shampoo (not a big priority since I have very little hair left) and a plastic-covered soap dish to carry inside the gym bag that I took with me when I swam laps at the pool where I was a member. I found the shampoo with no trouble, but had no luck with the soap dish. I spied a middle-aged woman wearing one of those bright blue vests and approached her. "Excuse me. Where do I find the plastic-covered soap dishes?" I asked. "They're in that area way over in that far section." Looking slightly annoyed at my having interrupted her, she waved her arm in the general direction, turned and walked away.

I copped an instant resentment. *What the hell kind of service was that?* I thought. She's supposed to show me where the item is, not dismiss me with vague directions and a wave of her arm. I was off to the front of the store to lodge a complaint. By the time I reached the customer service desk, I was already in a fine lather. I maintained my composure as I asked the young woman behind the counter if the store manager was available. "Just a moment sir, I'll call him." She smiled. She put down the phone and assured me that he would be there momentarily. As I waited my irritability increased. I start shuffling my feet and glaring at my watch. *Don't these people know how valuable my time is and how important I am? I've waited for at least 10 minutes by my calculations, It was only three minutes in real time.* Now I'm thinking that *I'll contact Walmart headquarters in Bentonville, Arkansas (Yeah, I know where it is). I'll have that clerk fired, and have this store shut down.*

I'm not exactly the personification of patience as I approach the customer service desk again. I ask the young woman, "What has happened to the manager who was supposed to address my complaint?" My tone of voice dripping with displeasure. This time she uses the store intercom instead of the phone. "Will the store manager please come to the customer service desk immediately? We have an irate customer here." I realize that I am that irate customer, and as she turns to reassure me that the manager is on his way, I notice her necklace. It's a thin gold chain and suspended on it is a small circle with a triangle in the center; it is the symbol of Alcoholics Anonymous. It catches me up short, making me aware of my horrible behavior. I don't want to, but I can't help it. "Are you in the program?" I ask.

"She smiles, "Why yes I am; I belong to the Circle Club and I just celebrated two years of sobriety. Are you a member, too?"

I've been behaving so badly I'm embarrassed to say yes, but I acknowledge that I am a member. "How long have you been sober?" She inquires.

I really don't want to tell her over 30 years, but I sheepishly answer anyway.

EAST OF APALACHICOLA

I was headed to New Orleans to visit friends who lived there and had recently gotten sober in A.A. I was negotiating a long sweeping curve on my BMW motorcycle on Florida State Route 98 which borders the Gulf of Mexico and offers spectacular views all the way through the panhandle when three F-16 fighter jets came swooping over my head at treetop level, scaring the daylights out of me. I'd had enough road for the day and started looking for a motel. I spotted a small place right off the highway and pulled in. It was a mom-and-pop operation and Mom was behind the counter in the office. "Do you have a vacancy ?" I asked. "Sure do, they're all vacant. Y'all on a motorcycle trip?" She asked. "I am and I sure do need a hot shower and a little rest." "Well, we got both." She swiped my credit card and handed me a room key and a receipt.

The room was Spartan to say the least, but it was clean and the water in the shower was hot. Somewhat refreshed, I decided to check on the nearest meeting, none were listed in my Eastern States A.A. meeting directory so I picked up the phone. Mom's voice came on the line from the front desk. "If you want to make a call you have to go through me to get an outside line." She explained. "No problem, could you please get me one?" I asked. I dialed the local Sheriff's office to find out where I might find a meeting. The deputy who answered said he'd have to find out and would call me back in a few minutes. I thanked him and hung up. The phone rang 10 minutes later and it was mom again. "I don't know what you're up to, but you've only been here a little over an hour and the Sheriff's office wants to talk to you." I assured her that I had called them for some information and they were just getting back to me. She probably listened in as the deputy gave me the location and directions to the meeting.

I arrived at the run-down cinder block building that was the A.A. club house and went inside. It was a small meeting, maybe 10 or 12 people at best. They welcomed me and I grabbed a cup of lousy instant coffee and sat down. It was one hell of a meeting!

A guy named Emil kept quoting scripture while curses from

several of the others flew around the room. At one point a very overweight *femme fatale* with black hair dyed so dark it looked like shoe polish objected to the vulgarity. One of the good old boys shot back, "Well, Miss Patricia, you sure wasn't concerned 'bout no vulgarity when Reverend Carl caught you givin' that newcomer a blow job in the men's room of the Congregational Church over on Tupelo Avenue, we was thrown out of there on account of you."

Miss Patricia blushed and smiled at the same time, "You hush now, Virgil, y'all will have this Yankee motorcycle rider wonderin' what kinda A.A. we got here." She was too late; I already was.

Now I'm thinking, *Where the hell am I?* Then I remembered what Richard had said all those years ago: "A lot of people in A.A. aren't wrapped too tight." Well, here was a room full of them. As we walked out at the end of the meeting, Miss Patricia asked me if I wanted to go get a coffee with her. I passed; hearing about her men's room 13th stepping (A.A. slang for one member seducing another) didn't exactly turn me on.

Next morning I asked mom if there was a local restaurant where I could get breakfast. "Take a left about a mile down the road and go down to St. Marks. They have a couple of places there that offer good local cooking."

I headed out, took the left, and drove into the tiny town of St. Marks. The town had obviously fallen on hard times. Rusted-out shrimp boats were tied to the docks and many of the buildings were dilapidated and storefronts were vacant. The two restaurants were almost side by side. I approached the one to the left where a man was sitting on the front steps smoking a cigarette. Before I could say anything he said, "We're all too hung over this morning, we ain't serving breakfast. Try the Riverside Café right over there." As I came up to the front of The Riverside a waitress in a blue and white checked uniform came out and began writing on the small blackboard next to the front door:

TODAY'S SPECIAL
Legs & Eggs

I complimented her on her handwriting and asked, "What are the legs?"

"Frog legs of course; come on in." She smiled.

The inside of The Riverside consisted of a small dining room that contained six old wooden picnic tables at which were seated a handful of regulars. I seated myself across from an older man who was sitting by himself at one of the tables. He had on a frayed and tattered denim shirt and a soiled baseball cap advertising Evinrude Outboard Motors perched on his head.

He nodded and smiled a silent good morning to me as I sat down. I couldn't help but notice that his teeth looked like tiny gray and black tombstones. It was one of the reasons why I sat at the table right in front of him. A plate of biscuits and a bowl of syrup were what he was having for breakfast. He kept soaking the biscuits in the syrup and sucking the sweet liquid off with a satisfied slurp each time he did so. My legs and eggs arrived and they were delicious.

As I finished up and was enjoying a second cup of coffee, I asked the old-timer what folks in St. Marks did for a living. With a straight face and a tone serious as a heart attack, he replied, "As little as possible." He paused, thought for a moment and then added, "A lot of us either go down to the 7-11 to get a beer to take the edge off or wait 'til the liquor store down the road opens up."

As I climbed on my bike and headed west, I said a silent prayer of thanks that I was on my way to New Orleans and not sucking on syrup soaked biscuits and waiting for the liquor store to open.

ALONE WITH
PICASSO AND DEGAS

I had been sober for 28 years when I worked at a world class museum that boasted one of the largest collections of Renoirs in the world. I had been there for three years when the museum was preparing for what would end up being the second most popular exhibit in its history: "Picasso Looks at Degas." The staff had been planning for over two years to bring it all together. Negotiations for the loan of paintings by both artists had been made with museums from the *Musée D'Orsay* in Paris to the Museum of Fine Arts in Boston and numerous other galleries and museums throughout the world.

Paintings had begun arriving on a daily basis for several weeks. As they arrived they were immediately taken to the museum's subterranean storage vault. The vault was really a huge, two-story, climate-controlled room fitted with racks to accommodate the crates that the paintings were shipped in.

The day had arrived when all of the crated canvases were moved into a secured upper level gallery, where they would be unpacked, inspected by our curators, insurance agents, and curators from the loaning museums. My assignment on that day was to stand at the closed door to the galley in my museum-issued gray slacks and blue blazer holding a clipboard listing the names of everyone who was authorized to enter. My instructions had been provided to me directly by the head of security: "If their name is not on the list, they do not get in. NO EXCEPTIONS!"

I knew our staff members, so I didn't have to check their badges as they arrived, but I had to scrutinize the badges and IDs of everyone else and put a check-mark next to their names. It was shortly after one o'clock when they all decided to have lunch in the museum's café.

In an instant I was left alone with masterpieces, a few of which I had seen in Paris, Boston and New York museums, many of the others only as illustrations in textbooks that I had studied while an art student. Here they were, propped against walls, lying on tables and workbenches all alone with me. As I walked among them I thought, *If these people knew what I was like during my drinking days, I would be the very last person they would leave in here with paintings valued in the millions of dollars.* My thoughts raced back to that meeting in my early sobriety. *I was untrustworthy and those alcoholics, knowing that, had trusted me with their money.*

Tears welled up in my eyes as I looked at the forlorn figures in *L'Absinthe* by Degas and I shuddered at where I might have been if it were not for the rooms and members of Alcoholics Anonymous.

ANGELA'S PHOTOGRAPH

I had begun my career as a photojournalist the same year I showed up at Alcoholics Anonymous. Some 20 years later I was at a Tuesday night speaker meeting. Afterwards I was thanking Susan, the out-of-town speaker I had just met, for making the commitment and doing such an excellent job of carrying the message. In the course of our brief conversation, I discovered that she had attended The Cooper Union School of Art in New York City. I had studied at The School of the Museum of Fine Arts in Boston. I told her that I had been an illustrator for 20 years with General Electric but now was working as a photographer.

"How interesting," Susan replied. "I teach a course in computer generated art and the school is looking for a photography teacher. Would you be interested in applying?"

I did apply and was offered the position which I accepted. It was an exclusive private school nestled in the beautiful Berkshire Hills of western Massachusetts. One of the final assignments I had given my students was to assemble a portfolio of black & white prints from the various categories I had assigned. After spending several weeks in the darkroom printing their photographs, my pupils sat in the classroom ready to critique their matted prints. One of the categories had required the students to submit a photograph depicting strength. As I flipped through the matted prints that were stacked neatly behind each other on an easel at the front of the class, some obvious interpretations were revealed: a tight shot of sinewy muscles that glistened with sweat as they pumped iron, a low angled perspective as a CAT D10 bulldozer's gigantic blade pushed a massive amount of soil and sod toward the camera, and steel girders that formed black linear divergent angles of strength against a muted gray urban skyline.

A few weeks earlier, Sarah, one on my students, had told me that she thought that a photograph of her grandmother would be an appropriate example of strength. "I think it just might be a different example of strength; by all means try it." I encouraged her.

I flipped to the next to the last matted 5x7 print in the stack on the easel and came to Sarah's photograph. It was a fine black and white print of an elderly gray-haired woman seated at a kitchen table. Her features were highlighted by sunlight streaming in from a window off camera, to her right. Her hands were clasped together and rested on the edge of the table. Illuminated by the sunlight was the tattoo on her forearm. It was the number that the SS had tattooed on her arm when, as a young woman, she had arrived at Auschwitz. "I think my grandmother, who endured so much and still survived the holocaust, is a quiet symbol of strength," her granddaughter offered.

The students sat in stunned silence, a few wiped away tears as the emotional impact of Sarah's photograph washed over them.

When I reverently removed Sarah's print from the easel, I was stunned by the final image that was displayed. Other than Susan and the headmaster of the school, I had completely maintained my anonymity as a recovering alcoholic. So when Angela's photograph appeared before the class the air rushed out of my lungs, I was stunned. It was a tightly composed image of a pair of man's hands resting on a table. The hands occupied a space between a copy of the Big Book of Alcoholics Anonymous and a cup of coffee. Angela's comment was short and simple in its eloquence: "I don't know very much about Alcoholics Anonymous, but it must be very strong. A.A. has given me back my father."

FINAL THOUGHTS

I have written this book sharing some of my life experiences as a recovering alcoholic to give readers an insight into the disease of alcoholism and evidence that recovery is possible.

If this copy has been read by you, who are not afflicted, I trust that the first part of the trilogy has given you some understanding of what it is like for the alcoholic who cannot stop drinking. Perhaps even the alcoholic in your life?

And, if you are, or suspect that you might be an alcoholic, I hope that the second and third parts of the trilogy have given you some hope. Now that there are many roads to recovery, all of the power and help you will need to recover from your disease awaits you. Alcoholics Anonymous has been the road that I have chosen. It is my personal opinion that A.A. works best for most.

If you have decided to ask for help; my best wishes go with you, and I drink (a club soda) to your success. "Bottoms Up!"

Paul C.
March 30, 2016

IN MEMORY

To paraphrase Charles Dickens; I grew up in what I believe were the best of times, and in my case one of the best of places. One of the advantages of being diagnosed with Pulmonary Fibrosis is that this disease has given me enough time to not only "Get my affairs in order," but to also write my final op-ed piece.

My parents Paul Arthur C. & Rita Evelyn C. (née Peat) gave me the gift of life in Adams, Massachusetts on Thursday, December 21, 1944. I am happy about having had a full life, and not despondent over having to die. I take great comfort and solace in memories of: movies at the Adams Theatre on Friday nights, sipping Cokes at The Crest, shooting pool at Billy Guerin's pool room, swimming at Peck's Falls, and in Anthony's Pool, and growing up in a small town that I have always loved and that has, in turn, loved me back.

I would like to thank the nuns at Notre Dame School in Adams for teaching me to read. They did however fail to teach me to write in the classic "Palmer Method." I was the only member of my eighth grade graduating class who did not receive a Palmer Certificate. My love of reading was nurtured by my parents as was my introduction to history by the first hardcover book I ever owned "Lee and Grant at Appomattox," by McKinley Kantor, a Christmas present from them in 1958.

The formal parts of my education took place at Adams Memorial High School and The School of the Museum of Fine Arts in Boston. I acquired the remainder of whatever wisdom and knowledge I have from being a voracious reader; and travel destinations that have included: a great many of these United States, Canada, France, Germany, Hong Kong, Singapore, Haiti and many other Caribbean islands.

I also want to thank Martha Nordstrom at Berkshires Week, Tom Morton, Ruth Bass, Helen Southworth at The Berkshire Eagle and Claire Piaggi at The North Adams Transcript who encouraged me as a writer and a photographer.

In my professional life , I worked as an illustrator with the Ordnance System Division of the General Electric Company, a construction worker, a wine steward (Sommelier if you prefer) a bartender, a photography teacher, co-owner along with Cheryl (my ex-wife and still a friend) of a successful photography studio, a photojournalist, op-ed columnist for the Berkshire Eagle and The North Adams Transcript, and finally as the author of 3 books. It appears that in my case, a career might have been somewhat a rather unimaginative idea.

I have been preceded in death by my parents, and my beloved younger sister Gail Sandra C.-Wellington. I am survived by my significant other, Susan Bradshaw of Melbourne, Florida, 2 children: my daughter Laurie LaVigne and her husband Mark of Adams and my son Adam and his wife Ruth Hon of Hong Kong, China, and by my Grandson Mark Therrien Jr. and his wife Caitlin of Stamford, Vermont, as well as several nieces and nephews.

I traveled extensively in my life, photographed and wrote about what I saw and experienced and was given the gift of being able to share it with others. I learned what I wanted to learn and loved who I wanted to love.

The love of my family and friends, has truly eclipsed all of the successes of my life. A special note of thanks to Richard Shea and Joel Bolshaw whose love, advice and guidance saved my life.

If reading this brings to mind a photograph that I took or a column that I wrote that touched your heart, or tickled your funny bone, or made you just say "What?" That's good enough for me.

Stop by at the services and re-tell stories I can no longer tell. Some of those stories may contain "R" rated material, parents of younger children should exercise caution.

And now it is time to give that gift of life back. Metaphorically speaking, I hope we shall meet again on the other side.

The TWELVE STEPS
of ALCOHOLICS
ANONYMOUS

1. We admitted we were powerless over alcohol—
   that our lives had become unmanageable.
2. Came to believe that a Power greater than ourselves
   could restore us to sanity.
3. Made a decision to turn our will and our lives
   over to the care of God *as we understood Him.*
4. Made a searching and fearless moral
   inventory of ourselves.
5. Admitted to God, to ourselves,
   and to another human being
   the exact nature of our wrongs.
6. Were entirely ready to have God remove
   all these defects of character.
7. Humbly asked Him to remove our shortcomings.
8. Made a list of all persons we had harmed,
   and became willing to make amends to them all.
9. Made direct amends to such people wherever possible,
   except when to do so would injure them or others.
10. Continued to take personal inventory and
    when we were wrong promptly admitted it.
11. Sought through prayer and meditation to improve our
    conscious contact with God, *as we understood Him,*
    praying only for knowledge of His will for us
    and the power to carry that out.
12. Having had a spiritual awakening
    as the result of these Steps,
    we tried to carry this message to alcoholics,
    and to practice these principles in all our affairs.

PUBLISHERS NOTE

Bottoms Up came to me through a series of chance encounters which led Cheryl C. to contact me about her former husband's work. I am honored to be trusted to bring Paul's legacy work to you. Since I did not have the opportunity to meet Paul, I toured his hometown of Adams, MA. This visit to his old haunts and speaking with some of the people who knew him well combined with reading his first book, *Time Pieces* helped me to feel closer to him. I am certain we would have become friends.

Paul had intended to publish Bottoms Up anonymously. However, I very much wanted to include his self-written obituary, so after much thought and discussion I have decided to list the author, in the A.A. tradition, as Paul C.

ABOUT HOTCHKISS PUBLISHING

Hotchkiss Publishing is founded on the simple belief, so well expressed by Nelson Mandela in his 1994 inaugural speech," as we let our own light shine, we unconsciously give other people permission to do the same." We hope that the words and ideas expressed by our authors remove fears, give hope, provide guidance, and open doors thought to be closed. May they assist you during your journey through this life to discover the greatness which lies within you.

Hotchkiss Publishing welcomes your comments and ideas for future projects. Please send them to:

Bill Ludwig
Hotchkiss Publishing
17 Frank Street
Branford, CT 06405
Bill@HotchkissPublishing.com